HARD TIMES COTTON MILL GIRLS

Personal Histories of Womanhood and Poverty in the South

VICTORIA BYERLY

ILR PRESS
New York State School of
Industrial and Labor Relations
Cornell University

© Copyright 1986 by Cornell University
All rights reserved

Cover design by Kathleen Dalton

Cataloging in Publication Data
Byerly, Victoria Morris.
   Hard times cotton mill girls.

   Includes index.
   1. Women textile workers—Southern States—Biography.
2. Women—Employment—Southern States. 3. Women—
Southern States—Economic conditions. I. Title.
HD6073.T42A132   1986   331.4'877'00922 [B]   86-20082
ISBN 0-87546-128-X
ISBN 0-87546-129-8 (pbk.)

Copies may be ordered from
ILR Press
New York State School of
Industrial and Labor Relations
Cornell University
Ithaca, New York 14851-0952

Printed in the United States of America
5 4 3 2 1

To Grandma

CONTENTS

MARRIAGE, MOTHERHOOD, AND WORK 75

BLACK WORKERS, WHITE MILL TOWN 125

SHIFTING FOR CHANGE 163

INTRODUCTION

Over the course of the past twenty years the writing of American labor history has undergone a significant transformation. Gradually persuaded by a proliferating ensemble of revisionist critics that a longstanding preoccupation with workers' institutions had deprived traditional scholars of a good understanding of workers themselves, today's labor historians generally agree that illuminating the previously neglected social and cultural history of the working class in America is an essential obligation of current scholarship.

In attempting to broaden and deepen their understanding of those aspects of workers' lives that narrowly focused institutional histories left unexplored, historians have recognized that conventional methods of analysis and traditional sources of information are often inappropriate or inadequate. This recognition has led many practitioners of the so-called new labor history to borrow from the social sciences techniques of inquiry and analysis that promised to unlock the rich potential of various types of "life records" from which the more intimate textures of working-class life and culture might be reconstructed. Yet as useful as such records have proven, they are usually only numerical representations that help to specify the generic circumstances rather than to disclose the emotional substance of workers' lives. Indeed, as the most astute of these historians realized that to know workers in the statistical aggregate was to know them only vaguely and generally, they have sought, often with remarkable resourcefulness and imagination, to retrieve the fragmentary transcript of the past left by workers themselves in the form of diaries, memoirs, family histories, and other writings reflective of their historical consciousness. And whenever practicable, historians have endeavored with increasing frequency and skill to augment the written record of workers' lives through oral interviews which, when they are conducted with proper sensitivity to the potential hazards that inevitably attend the exploitation of personal memories refracted by time and circumstance, afford an affinity with the past that is as dynamic and compelling as any that "outsiders" are likely to experience.

In the pages that follow, Victoria Byerly demonstrates the singular utility of oral history as a means of illuminating a working-class subculture whose interior has remained inaccessible to labor historians armed with traditional research methods and captive to conventional concerns. The richly textured portrait of southern working-class women that emerges from the personal reminiscences that follow testifies to the special value of oral interviewing as a vehicle for historical inquiry. It also reveals that one need not be a scholar, and weighted down with the intellectual and professional baggage the term implies, in order to use and profit from the inherently democratic techniques of oral history.

Victoria Byerly is not a conventional scholar, and despite the interest this book is likely to hold for serious students of women's history and working-class culture, her inspiration to produce it did not derive from the didactic impulse that typically actuates scholarship. Hers is a far more personal motive, one born out of a keen desire both to understand the regional culture that imprinted itself so indelibly on her own consciousness and to document in irreducible form a unique sisterhood of hardship and struggle forged in the textile mill villages of the Carolina Piedmont by the intersection of class and gender within the industrial continuum of the New South.

In the service of this highly personal and unashamedly passionate venture, Byerly has enlisted the plain-spoken and ingenuous recollections of twenty remarkable women. And although they are white and black and old and young, and unarguably distinctive and incomparable in all the ways that individual personality dictates, the common denominators of their lives—poverty, region, mill work, feminine culture—somehow subordinate individuality to commonality. Even race, that most central and immutable determinant of southern history, seems curiously diminished in its power to dispel the sense of solidarity and continuity these personal histories project.

The necessarily idiosyncratic character of the stories that comprise this book discourages broad generalizations about the place of women in the evolving industrial culture of the New South. They are nevertheless authoritative commentaries on the human trauma resulting from the fundamental changes in lifestyles, sex roles, and work patterns that accompanied the textile industry's inexorable economic subjugation of a region whose impoverished agriculture left its inhabitants unable and unwilling to defend their preindustrial heritage. By turns touching and trivial, instructive and bewildering, grim and funny, inspiring and disheartening, these stories offer in combination what is conspicuously absent from even the most competent and conscientious historical scholarship: a vivid sense of the profound and enduring importance of the commonplace.

That is not to say, however, that what Byerly discloses through her affectionate questioning of these women is prosaic or humdrum. Their individual and collective triumph over the despair that chronic powerlessness invites reveals an authentic, if private and unheralded, form of heroism to which the working poor in America have always been called. And more pertinent to current debates concerning the historical interaction of class and gender, there is running through these interviews a continuous thread of nascent feminism that expresses itself both in an irrepressible, if at times ambivalent, resistance to male hegemony and in a distinctly political orientation toward mill work that nurtured an appreciation of collective action even when it failed to breed a durable strain of unionism.

Finally, this is a book of rare value if for no other reason than because it provides a welcome antidote to the sophistical and intellectually enervating impression we too often indulge that history is somehow larger than the individual lives that populate it. J. M. Barrie, the celebrated author of *Peter Pan*, wrote: "If we unlock the rooms of the far past we can peer in and see ourselves, busily occupied in beginning to become you and me." Think of Victoria Byerly as an accomplished locksmith who has opened a seldom visited room of labor's past and ushered us into the presence of twenty of its most interesting and knowing residents.

Cletus E. Daniel.

A WRITER RETURNS HOME

My great-grandmother Mary Frances was a good Christian woman and the mother of twelve children. My great-grandfather Cicero was a hard-working, hard-drinking man who nourished his family on the harvest of his rented land and nourished his spirit on corn liquor. Mary Frances was middle aged when she gave birth to her last child and she finally gave up on Cicero. She and the children moved to town and she went to work in the new Amazon Cotton Mill. Eventually all ten of her surviving children followed her to the Amazon, as did their children and their children's children. When I went to work in the mill in 1967, four generations of women in our family had, all together, worked around four hundred years in the mill.

My grandmother Iola Mae married my grandfather Lacey at age fourteen, three years after she had gone to work in the Amazon. Like Cicero, Lacey was a hard-working man who loved his family but, also like Cicero, his love of corn liquor was what did him in. He was killed in a drunken brawl over the profits of a moonshine haul in 1948. Six months after he died, my mother, Clara Mae, gave birth to me. She was seventeen. Mama tells me Grandma said, "That's the ugliest baby I've ever seen," when she first saw me. Iola Mae then raised me as a favorite grandchild, alongside my Aunt Willa Faye, who is three years older than I.

Iola Mae never saw one day of schooling, so when I graduated from high school, the first one in all those generations to do so, she was proud of me. Yet for lack of a better alternative in our small southern town of Thomasville, North Carolina, I resigned myself that summer to following my family's tradition of mill work. On the one hand I was eager to find out what it was really like in the mill since I had heard about it all my life. I knew it was hard work and I wanted to see if I was tough enough to make it like everybody else. On the other hand, I was scared of getting trapped in the mill for the rest of my life. Having an education and all, I had other dreams.

That June I went to work in the mill. Like many of the women in this book, I was terrified my first day. Not so much because of the noise or the lint or even the heat: I was terrified that when that mill gate shut, it would never open for me again, and I would be stuck in the mill for the rest of my life like the three generations of our family before me.

My work in the mill was turning the cuffs down on little girls' socks. It was the next person's job to pack them in plastic. I had to turn thousands of socks a day before I could make the production quota. Any less and I would be out of a job. Everyone arrived a few minutes early in the morning and cut lunch a few minutes short to be ready to go when the whistle blew. At the sound of the whistle it was a race with the clock as I stood using every part of my body to move rhythmically back and forth to keep the pace required for production.

I was not very good at sock turning. My boss, a skinny guy in a white shirt and tie, was forever coming over to tell me that my work was sloppy and not fast enough. Finally I asked to be moved to the next row of sock turners beside Mable, a woman who had worked in the mill turning socks for more than thirty years. The precision with which Mable performed her job was incredible, and I strained to keep up with her. My work became faster but remained sloppy.

In late July I received a letter from a scholarship committee at my high school that said they had arranged for me to attend a small Appalachian college, and had managed to find me a grant and a work-study job to cover the one thousand dollar-a-year tuition. My family was too stunned to speak, but somehow I was not surprised. Somehow I just knew that I wasn't meant for the mill. I gave my notice at the mill the next day and said I would work on for a week—I only made it through three more days, though, before I walked out intending never to return.

The idea for *Hard Times Cotton Mill Girls* came to me in 1979 when as a staff member of a scholarly journal in Cambridge, Massachusetts, I proofread the galleys for a book on northern textile workers. Later when I learned that so little literature on southern textile workers existed, I felt cheated that my cultural heritage had not been taken seriously by historians. I began collecting data on southern textile workers with the idea that I might go back South and try my hand at oral history.

I was twenty-nine years old, unemployed, and living on a weekly check of sixty dollars when I returned to North Carolina in early spring 1980 with my tape recorder. I moved in with my grandmother who lived on the edge of the Amazon Cotton Mill village. She fed me and kept me in cigarettes throughout my stay. My mother, Clara Thrift, took me to K-Mart and bought my first supply of tapes and a two-drawer cardboard file cabinet. My sister Donna Smith loaned me a plastic typewriter she had received for Christmas one year, and my aunt Willa Faye Burchette loaned me a child's bicycle for transportation. I set up shop in my grandmother's house in the back bedroom, using her old pedal sewing machine as a desk, and began.

Grandma still worked in the cotton mill on the second shift and I was instructed not to mess up the house or dirty dishes while she was at work—just as she had instructed my aunt Willa Faye and me when we were growing up together in this same house. Because of these restrictions and Grandma's insistence on calling my work "playing school," I would have to wait until four o'clock, when she left for work in the mill, before I dared to spread out my papers to work. Then as midnight approached, the time of her return, I would scurry around picking up my "messes" and shoving them under the bed, very much as I had always done in her house.

I had been a happy child living in my grandmother's house in the Amazon Cotton Mill village, but when I was seven years old my family moved to another town. Though my mother continued to work in the textile industry, we moved into a neighborhood where I came in contact with people who were not mill workers. It was at this point that I began to feel ashamed of my background because I realized how poorly mill workers lived. We used out-houses instead of indoor toilets; we lived on beans and potatoes; we wore different clothes; and when the heels came off our shoes we hammered the nails down and went on wearing the shoes. In the mill village, where everyone lived this way, I had never thought anything about it. I didn't even know we were poor. But when we moved, I felt surrounded by people who seemed incredibly wealthy and who made me feel terribly inferior because of the clothes I wore, the way I talked, and the food I ate.

When I returned, after talking to hundreds of mill workers, I began to reconstruct a feeling of belonging that I had felt only as a small child, and I began to see the struggles of these people in a very different light. I realized that I had never been really poor. In fact, those mill workers whom I had known as a child seemed to be reaping the modest rewards of their lifetime strug-gles: they had homes—some quite cozy—indoor plumbing, and food to eat. The streets had been paved and children now played softball with real bats instead of sticks.

Life in southern mill towns is still not an easy life. Johnny Mae Fields told me that in Kannapolis, where she works in Cannon Mills*—recently purchased by Los Angeles businessman David Murdock—everybody is under pressure now. "Everybody is upset all the time, you know, weeping and gnashing teeth and going on all the time. Now Murdock is a businessman from the top of his head to his toes, and I don't think he cares what color you are, he just doesn't regard mill workers as human beings. He wants the job done, like he wants it done, and when he wants it done. And if you don't do it, I don't care what your job is, you can get out. So you find people with long faces feeling like they're working too hard—too much for too little."

*Now owned by Fieldcrest Mills

Despite their struggles, mill women maintain that they like their work because the mill is their life; it is what makes them who they are, gives them a lifestyle they are proud of. However, this is not without an awareness that their wages are among the lowest in the United States. This pride is not without the knowledge that the work they do is hard work that can be dangerous and over the years even prove to be fatal. They are familiar with the union-busting tactics of the textile industry. They know it is a runaway shop that came south after unionization of northern mills, and that East Asian textiles currently represent a formidable competitor to the southern mill owner. In Kannapolis, mill workers who had been laid off were recently rehired at a lower wage to work solely at sewing local labels over Taiwanese labels. The risk of organized protest is that the American textile industry will leave the South for the Asian Third World, where another hardworking, eager, and cheap labor force of women and children awaits it. In spite of the risks, however, southern mill women continue a tradition of determined struggle—for better wages, better working conditions, a cotton dust standard and compensation for brown lung disease, and, most of all, for a life of dignity.

FROM FARM TO FACTORY

The Civil War not only destroyed the southern economy but left the South itself, where most of the war was fought, in ruins. For southern leaders, who vowed that the South would rise again and sought to restore white supremacy and economic stability, industrialization was now an imperative, and the southern gentry devised a plan called the Cotton Mill Campaign. Cotton, the South's most abundant agricultural resource, was an obvious target for industrialization. Until this time cotton grown in the South had been transported to northern cotton mills for processing. Building cotton mills in the South would eliminate transportation costs, make use of an eager and cheap labor force—white sharecroppers who had been living on the edge of survival for generations—and increase profits. The mill doors would be shut to black workers, who would have no other alternative than to take the place of the impoverished sharecroppers, become servants, move north, or die. In addition to the complete disempowerment of the newly freed slaves, the South's plan also promised to bankrupt one of the North's leading industries—that of cotton manufacturing.

By the turn of the twentieth century, the Cotton Mill Campaign was in full swing. Cotton mills were in operation throughout the South, but concentrated in the Piedmont region of North Carolina. As anticipated, the dirt farmers jumped at the chance to be engaged in wage labor. Southern entrepreneurs were most interested in hiring women and children, the cheapest laborers, freeing the man of the household to continue farming. In an area where families of six to twelve children were very common, a combination of wage labor and farming promised an easier way of life. In addition, mill houses—plain white clapboard houses with indoor kitchens, up to five or six rooms, and electric lights—could be rented on the grounds of the mill for a few dollars a month. This opportunity was attractive to people who had been living in one- or two-room homes without plumbing or electricity.

The cotton mill village was like one big white family closed off to the external world. Rows and rows of white clapboard houses lined dirt roads leading to the mill, while the mill owner lived some distance away in a mansion.

Workers, mostly women and children, labored sixteen hours a day for wages that were just enough to pay rent on their mill houses and their bills at the general store. Mill workers survived primarily on food grown in their own gardens. Mill owners not only encouraged child labor, they insisted upon it. Some mill villages provided schools, but most did not, and the majority of this first generation of mill workers grew up illiterate. The church was usually built on land owned by the mill which also provided its financial support. Thus sermons frequently followed the theme of hard work, deprivation, and suffering as the path to salvation. Mill owners regarded their relationship to mill workers as a paternal one and in some cases actually provided the services of a small independent community such as limited medical care, sewing, cooking and canning classes, and various recreational activities including softball teams and contests for the best gardens. The Cone village in Greensboro, North Carolina, provided coal for heating which was delivered to each mill worker's door. At Christmas-time, free hams and turkeys, Christmas trees, and a toy or two for the children were handed out. In the beginning, carpenters were hired to maintain the houses. One mill worker in the Amazon mill village remembers:

> When they installed toilets in the mill houses, the workers were always stopping them up with newspaper. This kept

Amazon mill house, 1911. Bertha Miller is the girl in a white dress standing on the porch.
Photo courtesy of Bertha Miller.

the carpenters so busy that the company finally decided to put a stop to that. So once a week they'd send a truck around with a load of toilet tissue and they'd give each house two rolls. You could see people lined up and down the street waiting for their toilet tissue.

The mill village system was meant to control all aspects of the workers' lives—from church to education to the welfare system. It is ironic, then, that it was the mill that actually gave the white southern woman her first taste of economic independence. Mill work provided her with the opportunity to join the American labor market, and to leave her home in the country and come to town to live in a boarding house and work for a wage. Some women gained independence from their husbands by finding a home in the mill village while their husbands stayed on the farm. In fact, hundreds of families left the farm, loading up their few belongings in wagons with a cow or mule in tow, and headed to the cotton mill. The mill was a more modern way of life, and it promised an opportunity to elevate oneself. But as the mill village developed, so did the mill owners' absolute control of the workers' cultural and institutional life.

By the late 1920s the mill owners' air of paternalism had all but completely eroded. Many southern mill owners had passed ownership on to their sons, who, endowed with their business degrees, focused on one concern: higher profits. The sense of community and family that mill workers had once felt disappeared. Services once rendered to workers were no longer available. Mill houses were sold or neglected. Community leaders began to brag about the passivity of the mill workers as a way of enticing northern industry, and mill workers began to feel their isolation from the community and contempt from the outside society. The mill village became shabby, and the life of the mill worker grew more desperate.

ANNIE VIOLA FRIES

High Point, North Carolina

I was born in 1921, September the twenty-seventh. There was twelve children in my family and I was the youngest. Two of 'em died and my mother raised ten—five girls and five boys. My grandparents were dead on both sides by the time I came along so I don't know either one. My mother never really knew her age—their home got burned up and the family Bible was lost. That's what she always told me so I really don't know how old she was. Now some of the older ones might know more about it. I think I came along when she was going through the change.

She was a little short woman, weak, plain; my mother was real plain. Kept the house always clean even with the crowd of kids that she had. We had cane bottom chairs, a wood table with a bench, but everything was clean—I can remember that. We scrubbed the floors with our brooms and Red Devil lye soap. We did all that. Me and my mama would go pick blackberries; wash, we'd wash clothes, and I'd hang them out, go to church, brush arbor meetings, they'd have that and we'd go to them. There'd be big old poles holding the sides up and they'd put brush on top for the roof and they'd hold religious services. Instead of having tents, they'd have that, and they'd call it brush arbor meetings. Anybody that'd come through with a tent, we'd go to that. I remember doing things like that with my mother. We didn't have a car and travel like that unlessin some of the older ones that was married and they had a car, now, they'd come and take us, but to have one at home we didn't.

My mother was religious and she'd take us to church. She couldn't read but she'd teach us what she knew—what people would read and preachers would preach—and she'd listen and then when we got up and could read she'd have us to read scriptures in the Bible to her. I read lots of scriptures to her when I came along and got to where I could read, you know. She'd ask me and I'd read it to her.

Now my father left. Well, I hadn't even started to school now when he left, I don't even remember what year it was. Some of the older ones might remember that now, but he left and he wasn't there with us. But he'd come by, he lived close by, and he'd come and get me and he'd take me on the wagon with him and I'd go on the wagon. He farmed, my daddy did. Sometimes I'd walk to the fields just to get to ride the horse to the barn 'cause I liked to ride the horse, and he'd let me do that. He had gentle horses and he'd put me up on one and I'd ride to the house. Then I used to go to the fields and hoe corn, used to help him, you know, and he'd come by on the wagon sometimes going to the mill to grind the corn to make flour, wheat, and stuff like that, he'd make cornmeal with the corn, and he'd come by going to the mill or going to town to get stuff and I'd jump up on the wagon and go with him and he'd buy me material to make me a dress or buy me a pair of shoes. Oh Lord, there were more horses and wagons than there were the old T-model Fords. That's about all there were. That was back in the thirties. I always did love my daddy. My mama never did teach me against him. She told us that he was our daddy and we was to love him. And I loved him, I really did, because if I'd get sick he'd come to the house to see me. That's the only time I can remember him coming to the house. If I'd be sick, Mama would let him come in to see me. If she'd see him coming up the road on the wagon or the horse, she'd call me and tell me he was coming, and I'd run out and find out where he was going, and if it was to town, see, I'd go with him. And he'd let me go with him.

I was born over at the old home place. They said I was born in that corner in the bed. Time I came along, see, they was having doctors and my mother had old Doctor Phillips, but they had their younguns at home, they didn't go to the hospital then. So my mother had me there in the house. It was just a three-room house. The kitchen was real big. The back room, we called it the back room, was a big old long room. Mama had four beds up in it: two on this side and two on this side, and at the end of the windows was an old timey trunk. Then up here sat an old cupboard that we kept our linen and things in. Then along here at the door sat her sewing machine. Then you go in and that was the fire room. She had a bed in there and a fireplace. We called it the fire room. It was the living room really. We sat in it. My mother always used the fireplace, we never had a heater. Then in the kitchen was the cook stove, that's what we had to heat with.

We had a bed in the fire room and I always slept out there with my mother. When my sister Bessie was home, if she was working out, she slept in that bed with us and I would sleep in the middle. That's the way we did it. In the back room, that was where all the boys and girls in my family slept when they was growing up, the boys had their side and the girls had their side. But see, some of the older ones, like Gene and Geneva and Emer, they were already married and gone, and I growed up with their kids. Their kids were more like my sisters and brothers than they were my nieces and nephews. When I went to school my nieces and I would wear the same clothes. We'd do things like that.

I just remember Bessie being at home. 'Cause I remember Bessie would come here in High Point and get her a job. Back then you couldn't buy a job, it was hard. So she came over here and kept house for people on the Highland Mill hill. She'd take me over with her sometimes. One time she brought me over and took me to town and bought me some little sandal shoes. I never will forget that. Then finally she got herself a job in the mill and went to work in there. See, that's how we lived, like that. Naturally Bessie would come home and give my mother money, board money she'd call it, but it was just really helping out.

When I got old enough I quit school and I went in the mill to help my mother. By that time my mother was sick and she wasn't able to do anything. So I went to work on the third shift. Come in of the morning and build fires in the old wood stove and cook breakfast and then go to bed and sleep that day and get up that evening, clean house, and help my mother. We had a little old girl to stay with my mother, because, see, when we went off to Maryland, we couldn't leave her by herself so we had this little old girl who stayed with her for two dollars a week and her board. We'd give her two dollars or five dollars a week and her board. That's the way we did it.

It was just me, Reevie, and Bessie at home that I can remember. I think I had it easier than the rest of my mama's younguns because, see, then the older younguns had got out of the way and then they was working and they'd help Mama with me. Like Bessie would give me things and Reevie would buy me things. He sent me to school and bought my books, shoes, clothes, and everything, he did. See if it hadn't been for my brother Reevie I probably wouldn't have got to went to school that much. I got to go to the seventh grade.

Mama wanted us to have an education, she really did, it would have tickled her if one of us had went and graduated. That would have thrilled her to death. It would have, because she wanted us to learn to read. She thought that was important because when she was a little girl, she told me about going to school and she said that she set rabbit guns, her mama was dead, see, and her sister and brother was raising her. She said she'd set rabbit guns and catch rabbits in them and cook it that night and pack her lunch to take to school the next day—what little she got to go. She could print just a little but she couldn't read or write. She'd just print a little bit, I remember that. I remember she said they were all just kids living on this farm in this house and they had to raise everything they had to eat. She said one time they didn't have nothing to eat. She said not even cornbread was in the house and she had to do without food for three days. They didn't eat nothing for three days. Then, she said, they just got up one morning and stood on their porch and she just thought, "Now, if I don't get something to eat today, I'll die." That's what she thought to herself, now, I've heard her tell it more than one time.

She said her sister Em or sister Sarey, I can't remember which one was the oldest, went over to a farmhouse over across the woods from them and borrowed a quart, now just think about it, a quart of cornmeal for them to eat that day 'til they could get food and have something. She said she brought it in and they couldn't wait for her to cook it so they just dipped in it and got them a mouthful, they was so hungry.

Both her mama and daddy were dead. Her mama had had measles and she got wet, went to get the horses to run them in the barn, and she got wet and had a backset and died. That was my grandmother and that's what happened to her and my mother was still little and that just left her brother and sisters. Her daddy was already dead. One of her sisters was grown and had gone to Winston-Salem to live and the others was at home, they hadn't gotten married yet, so Sarey and Em and her brother was raising her. These kids was working this little old farm and they just didn't have nothing to eat at that time. They was waiting on the crops to grow in the garden so they could have stuff. When it did come in they'd can and do in the summer so they'd have it in the winter. Then they'd catch rabbits and wild stuff to eat. That's the way they did.

Anyway, they raised her, and then Em got married and Sarey got married to my daddy's cousin. They was cousins some way. Then my mother went to live with a woman up in Winston to work at Freeze's Cotton Mill. She was just a youngun then 'cause that was before she was married and she was just a youngun when she married my daddy. So she went up there and got her job, but her sister Nettie got sick and Mama couldn't stay and had to come back to live with Sarey and that's when they introduced her to my daddy. Mama had met a boy up there in Winston that she liked, but she couldn't go with him 'cause they had to come back down here to live. So she met my daddy. So Sarey, now, I've heard my mother tell this, Sarey told her that she had to marry my daddy cause he was twelve years older than her and a good provider and he could give her a home and could provide for her.

So my mother married my daddy and had twelve younguns. I

have no idea how old she was because that was after she had worked in the mill and back then you could go to work in the mill around eight or nine. But I have no idea how old she was when she got married. I mean, she had to have been of age to have children. She could have been thirteen or fourteen when she had her first baby. She had us kids about a year and a month apart. Every one of us is like that. I've heard Mama tell it, that she wouldn't no more than wean one than she was pregnant with anothern. I've heard her tell it. And my daddy, he'd just take us and put us right out in the field to work. He believed in that. But I was the youngest, so I didn't have to do like the older ones. That's why I said I think I had it easier than the others. I really do, and see I got to go to school where the others—Geneva, Gene, Emer, Clarence, Bash, Clyde—none of them got to go to school. So I was fortunate in that way.

I liked school, when I got to go. I went to Fairgrove. They had the Fairgrove School by the time I came along and Reevie and I went there. A lot of the kids I went to school with were from Silver Valley, down there way down in that section, down 109 South, down near the Liberty Church, they come from that far. They were farmers' kids. That is, their parents would work in the factories and raise what food they eat. And a lot of 'em worked in the mills. What didn't work in the cotton mills worked in the shops, the furniture factory. Some just farmed and didn't work out nowhere. Like my daddy. Some of the farmers were into farming big, and they had big old houses and nice things. They was on the Board at the schoolhouse. You know what I mean, now, them kind. They was the good farmers, I'd call 'em. But little old truck patches like my daddy's were dirt farmers, we'll call it that. Now they was the ones that didn't have much.

We didn't have much to wear and no shoes. If you did have a pair of shoes, you'd have a hole in the bottom of them. Back then you could buy cotton material for five cents a yard and make your own dress, a little old plain thing. My mother would get flour sacks and sewed up many a dress for me to wear to school. I can remember it just like it was yesterday. Now that's how I got my clothes. I never had a new coat. An old man would come by, we called him Tradin' Charles Lambeth. He's dead now. But he'd come by and he'd sell you used coats and my mother would buy coats from him for fifty cents or a dollar. If it was a good one then we'd have to pay him a dollar for it. But I've known her to just give him fifty cents for a whole coat for me to wear. Yeah, I remember old Tradin' Charles Lambeth, here he'd come peddlin' old coats and clothes. Mother would go through them and if there was anything to fit me and I needed it, see, she'd get it for me. But if I didn't need it, I didn't get it, if I had one. See, you had just one thing and you wore it to school and to church too. I didn't really have as much clothes as the other kids, I remember. Well, some of 'em we lived better than them 'cause some of 'em was really right down dirt poor, lived in little old shacks. I never remember going to bed hungry. We always had beans and po-tatoes. We had flour and she'd make biscuits and jelly. So we lived pretty good and see, too, the kids, the older kids, had gone to work and they'd help my mother out.

I remember Reevie getting groceries and things and Mama buying bananas and I could have a banana to take to school. Peanut butter and crackers is what you'd take to school back then. I remember Mama would buy a big old box of crackers and a big old jar of peanut butter on pay days. That would be our school lunch for the week, me and Reevie. And if she had a biscuit or something, maybe she'd put us in a biscuit. If we didn't have crackers she'd put in a biscuit, but we'd be ashamed to pull the biscuit out because, see, everybody else would be eating white bread. We was ashamed of the biscuit. The kids would make fun of us. Back then they'd make fun of you if you came to school a little more raggedy than them. Then I had long hair and the rest of the kids had short hair, and I can remember them pulling my pigtails and making fun of me. Just little old mean kids, just a picking, they didn't mean no harm. I had some good teachers and everyone seemed to like me. I never did have a mean teacher. Even Miss Thomas, oh, everybody thought she was the meanest teacher, she'd stomp through the halls and yell and holler, and they'd say, "Oh, she's a mean one." I always heard that and when I got her grade, well, I couldn't have asked for a better teacher and I liked her, I really did.

After a few years they put in cafeterias in schools. We used to not have any and you'd have to carry your lunch, but then they went to giving you a hot meal. You could get a bowl of soup for a nickel or a plate lunch for a dime. I can remember that and after dinner what milk was left the underprivileged kids could go in and have. And I used to get choosed to go in there and drink the chocolate milk. Then you didn't get chocolate milk and that was a treat as a child. We had milk at home because we had a cow, but we didn't have no chocolate milk. So I'd grab me one of them little cartons and it tasted so good. If there was no chocolate left you'd get the plain milk and it tasted good because it was pasteurized. Back then we would just drink it right from the cow at home. That's the way we did. That milk at school, it just tasted so different and so good. If a child was real poor, dirt poor, they'd try at the school to get them something to eat or report that child to the welfare, and then the welfare would give them clothes to come to school and see that they had something to bring to eat.

The Hamiltons and the Clodfelters, their daddies was in business and they had these big old houses and they were the rich children and they drove the school buses. They was nice to us. I reckon their mothers would have killed them if they had been ugly to us poor kids. See Fisher Ferry Street and down that way used to be nice with big old houses. When I growed up, Fisher Ferry was it. The Clodfelters used to live up on the hill in a big old house that sat on the corner. They lived there and they had one girl. Now they was what I'd call rich. They were it, they were the tops. Virginia was her name and she went to Fairgrove School. And dress! They dressed her in the best. The house had a stone porch around it. Now they was the people who was the leaders at our school. They was nice to us, though. We used to go down there to wait for the school bus and she used to let us come in there where it was warm and wait.

But just a few had a little more than the others. Most everybody else was poor like us. But nobody seemed to be that snooty, as long as you was halfway decent and clean. Where we lived was a bunch of rented houses and people would move in and out and I'd play with different ones. Sometimes I'd play with the Helplers' children. We'd play with our dolls, me and Doris, and build playhouses down through them woods. We'd jump rope, jump plank, roll tires, climb trees, we'd just do everything. We were just normal children. Her mama and daddy were cotton mill workers. They worked in the Amazon.

I grew up near the Amazon Mill village, and by the time I came along half my brothers and sisters had married and were living in the mill village. They had nice houses for next to nothing for rent, had running water, bathrooms inside, and at home we had an outside toilet and a well to draw our water. So they lived good in the mill village. I thought it was good that the mill company would fix something for you like that. See when they got married and left home and got a house like that, I guess it was like moving into heaven for them.

When I turned a teenager, Mama got sick and my brother was buying my books, and clothes, and he was just running everything. Then he got married to Suny, and then it was different after he got married. Mama said that we couldn't expect as much 'cause Reevie had to have some of his money. Reevie paid five dollars, Suny paid five dollars, and I paid five dollars to Mama after I went back to work. That was our board money. Mama would run our house on that back then. Of course Reevie helped out more, he bought Mama's medicine and stuff like that. By the time I was a teenager I felt like I should help out, Mama being sick and everything. Then too I was old enough that I wanted things too, like clothes. I wanted to have my own things and didn't want to be begging somebody all the time for stuff. And I didn't have nobody to help me in my lessons 'cause it was getting harder and harder every day. So I just told Mama that I'd quit school and go to work.

I looked and hunted for a job everywhere. This was back in

the thirties and you just couldn't buy a job. It was just after the Depression, this was, so I went down to the Amazon and they weren't hiring, and I went to the Jewel Mill and they weren't hiring, and all the hosiery mills, and none of 'em were hiring. So my mother took me and went to the Amazon and Curl Lee was the big wheel over there. He took me in the office and sat me down and my mama told him—I sat right there and heard every word—she said, "Now this is my last girl, and you know all my children, girls and boys, have been working in this mill for years and they still here a working and this is my last one and she's a girl and I don't want to send her off from home. I want to keep her home, she's all I've got to keep me and I want to keep her here as long as I can. She needs a job so she can help me 'cause my last boy just got married and he's still home living with me but I need this one to go to work." And you know what? He hired me. He said, "You hired. Be down here at a certain time to go to work." And I did.

This man, he was a boss man, he didn't want to hire me, but Curl Lee made him hire me. So he said, "Who do you want to learn ya?" And Bessie had told me to ask for Callie Luther, so I did, and Callie Luther taught me to wind. I believe she's still alive. Her and Bessie lived in mill houses side by side. And when I went to learn they didn't pay me one dime. You went for weeks without pay. They put me on sides* by myself after I had got learnt and I had worked for about a week and a half, something like that, without no payday. Then one night he came around and he said, "Now Annie, I'm going to put you on the payroll," and that thrilled me to death. From then on I was on the payroll. But see, I had to learn all them weeks with no money at all, had to go in there

---

* spinning machines are set up in long rows that the worker tends by walking along and piecing up the broken ends. The number of sides a worker is given indicates the number of spools she is spinning or winding.

every day and then when it got to where I could go by myself
and leave Callie and work sides by myself, I still had to work
without money. Ain't that awful? We mill workers come a long
ways.

I remember I made twelve dollars a week. And I went and
bought a living room suite. We had never had a living room suite
in our house and I went up to Houghton's up there in town and
bought our first living room suite. I paid one dollar a payday on
it. That made the payments. If I had to be out because work got
slack I'd pay fifty cents to make my payments until I got that
thing paid for. It was covered in that blue velvet, a blue velvet
thing, and oh, I was so proud. I'd fix that thing up there in front
of the fireplace and Mama was as proud of it as I was. She'd have
prayer meetings and had the preacher over to see that beautiful
living room suite. I'm not kidding, I'm not stretching it. The Lord
knows that's the truth.

See, then you did that way, you didn't have a whole bunch of
stuff. Back then you just had cane bottom rockers and cane bottom
chairs, and you'd sit around the fire and that was your sitting
room. I just told Mama that I wanted to buy a living room suite
'cause I wanted to date and bring the boys in and sit and have
something that looked nice. And she said, "Well, we'll see what
we can do." So we went up to Houghton's and she helped me
pick and choose and we found out the price of it and paid two
dollars down. That's what we done. See, you couldn't go to the
bank and borrow money if you just owned a lot and a house like
we did. My daddy built the house, that's how we got that. And
it had never been painted, so we painted it and Mama had a
porch built on, 'cause we always wanted to sit out there and rock
in the summer. So she had a carpenter come over and build a
front porch. And me and Reevie was working in the cotton mill
so we paid for it.

KATIE GENEVA CANNON

Kannapolis, North Carolina

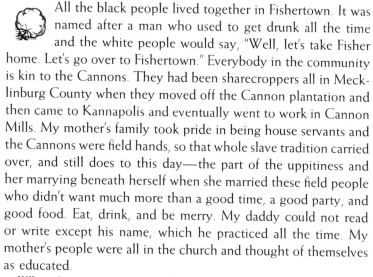 All the black people lived together in Fishertown. It was named after a man who used to get drunk all the time and the white people would say, "Well, let's take Fisher home. Let's go over to Fishertown." Everybody in the community is kin to the Cannons. They had been sharecroppers all in Mecklinburg County when they moved off the Cannon plantation and then came to Kannapolis and eventually went to work in Cannon Mills. My mother's family took pride in being house servants and the Cannons were field hands, so that whole slave tradition carried over, and still does to this day—the part of the uppitiness and her marrying beneath herself when she married these field people who didn't want much more than a good time, a good party, and good food. Eat, drink, and be merry. My daddy could not read or write except his name, which he practiced all the time. My mother's people were all in the church and thought of themselves as educated.

When I was growing up, there was only one paved road and that was our road, Charlie Walker Road. White people lived at one end and all the black people lived in the middle. At the other end of the road, a white man lived in a big house right in the curve. His name was Charlie Walker. So they said, "Well, what we going to name this road?" Charlie Walker Road, that's what they called it. He used to walk down his road all the time. We'd say, "There goes Mr. Charlie Walker." Our house had a fence around it, between it and the other houses on each side. Daddy's baby brother, Uncle Sam, lived next door to Grandpa across the street, who lived next door to Aunt Emma. So you had a whole row of families and everybody went back and forth running between yards all the time. Fishertown had about thirty families in it. That was the Cannons and their offsprings.

My grandmother's name was Cora Witherspoon Cannon. I loved my Grandmother Cora. She was a sharecropper and had married a man by the name of Dan Cannon. His family had been slaves on the Cannon cotton plantation which later became Cannon Cotton Mills. They had twelve or thirteen kids. She had one by the sharecropper so there was one white child in the family. Grandma Cora was a tall woman, like an African queen, and tenderhearted.

Grandma Cora Cannon lived right across the road from us, and because my father Esau was an identical twin with his brother Jacob, they were like the favorites. They were the only ones that didn't drink. Several of my aunts and uncles have died of alcoholism. The twins were the favorites and so their children were the favorites, and we were the only ones on the whole Cannon side of the family who went to Scotia Seminary.

Grandma Cora didn't believe that we had to share every stick of chewing gum like my mother did, so going to her house was always like a splurge. She had bottled drinks and she'd have two or three kinds of meat at one meal, while we only believed in having one chicken. We'd have one chicken for nine people. She believed that nobody should ever be hungry. She didn't stress style or education, she stressed the way you shared your love and wealth with people. Who you are, your status, was shown by having food, good food. She always had three meats and always had googobs of dessert, and you didn't have to share. To share was to show poverty. Everybody could have their own, and that was totally against my mother's teachings. I just loved Grandma Cora, and because we were Esau's kids she had a great deal of respect for us too. We didn't get to go over there often even though she just lived across the road from us. My mother kept saying we were different from the rest of the Cannons. We were

Fishertown, Kannapolis, in the 1950s. Katie Geneva Cannon stands at the far right. *Photo courtesy of Katie Geneva Cannon.*

the educated side. She wanted us to be more like her side of the family.

Grandma Cora would say to Grandpa Dan, "Dan, go upstairs and knock Rufus down three times." So he'd go upstairs and you'd hear BOOM, BOOM, BOOM. Then he'd come back downstairs and say, "Cora, what did I do that for?" Rufus was my daddy's brother and he was always getting into trouble, stuff like stealing meat out of the brothers' and sisters' freezer. See, my grandmother was taller than my grandfather, and whenever she didn't get her way then she'd fake a heart attack. Then we'd call the white doctor to come out to the black community, Dr. Nolan, and try to coax him to come. Everybody would be on alert. "Well, is she living or dying?" She always lived, just hadn't got her way. She was spoiled. My family took care of her until she died when I was eight.

My mother lived with the Cannons when she and my daddy first got married. They never liked my mother. They didn't think she was good enough for my father. He being so special to his brothers and sisters, Mama wasn't light-skinned enough. Uncle Jacob married a high-yellow woman, so three of his kids are very light-complexioned. Then we came along dark-skinned with nappy hair. That wasn't the way it was supposed to be. Whenever Daddy and Mama would argue about something, he would always go over across the street to his mother's and that would upset my mother so much.

The Cannons partied a lot and two of my aunts were bootleggers. The Cannons were always carousing and driving into ditches on Saturday night, cutting up, and my mother just had greater dreams for us. Our county was totally dry, so you had to go up to Rowan County and they'd get about four or five cases of beer to sell. They'd get it for thirty-five cents a can and sell it for seventy-five cents a can. People would come to my aunt's house and buy beer, chitlins, pickled eggs, and hot sausages. She'd have this food all cooked up and so people would buy food and drink all night long. They'd have liquor too. The whole house became a jukejoint on Friday night. This was Aunt Tot's and Aunt Sis's houses. Their houses were spotless during the week and Aunt Tot's house was the homeplace, that's where Grandpa and Grandma Cannon lived. Everybody was always over there, all the grandkids, all the brothers and sisters and sisters-in-law. You'd come home and eat and you'd have to go over by the house and see about the folk. It was a big house with a lot of cushion chairs in the living room and in the den. Then, it was the biggest house I knew. The house would stay the same when the different clientele came. There was an upright piano and there were these big overstuffed arm chairs like World War II furniture. In every space in the house there was a couch or a chair. Lots of pictures that had a blue and green tint to them of family people, but I never knew who they were. Later on there were always pictures of Martin Luther King, Jr., and the Kennedy brothers. A lot of knick-knacks, glass horses, glass chickens, ashtrays, and vases. Everywhere there was a place to sit and a table top with doilies. Now Aunt Sis had a serious jukejoint. Hers was down in the basement with tables, a juke box, and a bar and stools, and there would be cushion chairs down there too. I always wondered why my mother never had scars. They all had scars where people had cut them, and I thought these scars were like African tribal marks. I used to think Ma was deprived because she didn't have any scars.

I loved my aunts. They were so kind to us. They were both heavy set, brown-skinned, and cuss, oh God, they could cuss. Go to worship on Sunday though and put beaucoup money in the church. They were so proud of us because we were Esau's kids. When we came around they would try to put on their best manners and they were always trying to feed us. "Eat, eat. We gon' get these little skinny kids to eat. Eat!" We weren't used to people shoving food at us like that. Most of the time, we'd get sick 'cause we'd overeat. Egg custard, pecan pie, pound cake, all the fried chicken you wanted, all the potato salad you wanted, all the green beans, pork chops, homemade biscuits all the time, butter, butter, butter, and buttermilk and cornbread with cracklin'. Always ate high on the hog. My mother was always into nutrition and had gone to the clinic and learned how to eat prunes and oatmeal, and that kind of food at my aunts' houses wasn't supposed to be good for us. My mother was very body conscious and she didn't want us to be fat. When we reached adolescence, she said, "Why can't y'all be petite? Why'd I have to have these big old grown girls?"

My other grandmother, Grandma Rosie, was born in 1882. She lived with us all my life until she died. Her name was Rosa Cornelia White Lytle. She had one sister named Anna. Because her mother, Polly, had died when Rosie was an infant, she was passed from relative to relative. Grandma Rosie was the smartest one in her class. She loved education, she loved reading, she loved writing and making things. One of her greatest prides was that she had never worked for a white person. Never in her whole life. She was ashamed that my mother worked as a domestic and that we were being trained to be domestics. She was just a very thrifty, ingenious woman who believed in her home. She crocheted, she sewed, made things from scratch—made her patterns out of newspaper—and all the curtains in her house had to be starched. Booker T. Washington and George Washington Carver had stayed in her home. Like, when famous black people would come through, they would have to stay with black people. Because she was Mr. Manuel's wife—that's what she always called her husband because he was seventeen years older than her—then her home was the centering place.

My grandfather's name was Emmanuel Lytle and my aunt described him as a Martin Luther King. He had worked and saved until he got his land. When the whites took his land he had a nervous breakdown. It was good bottom land and they wanted it so they just took the deed and said he didn't own any land. So he came home one day and said, "I'm done for." And that was it, he broke. He couldn't fight it. He couldn't get his land back, so he had a breakdown, got pneumonia, and died. My great-grand-mother Mary had instilled in him how much it meant that he was her only free child, so to lose that land was to lose his freedom. He couldn't deal with it. That was in the 1920s when that happened.

My grandfather had ten children by his first wife and then he married Rosa and they had ten children. Five of hers lived. His first ten children were almost as old as she. Rosa was a kind mother who mothered these stepchildren as well as her own.

After all her children had left home, my mother brought her back to our house, where she lived until she died. She was the one who greased our faces everyday with Vaseline and combed our hair. She was a very gentle woman. She had a hump on her back, a wind is what they called it. She had always had it. She had crippled hands from arthritis, but I didn't even know they were deformed until sometimes children wouldn't take candy from her. She'd scratch her hair, "Oooh," she'd say, "it's like lice up here." So we'd all of us get in there and be scratching her head. She would let me comb her hair until it was real soft. I've gotten the comb tangled in her hair so many times and we'd have to cut that part out. She'd never get upset. She'd say, "It's all right, it's all right." It would do us such an honor to comb her hair, put her stockings on when she got out of the bed, grease her legs, and walk her to church. I learned a lot about patience, a lot about just what it means to be a human being.

My Grandma Rosa was a thinker, and she used to make us pronounce words correctly. If we said, "I wone some mo'," "Mo'?" she asked, "Morrrre!" She was always correcting us. She had this little proverb, "Be in the ring if it don't mean a thing, just be there." She cited poetry all the time and she was interested in our dreams. I would sit and read the Bible with her every night and she taught me how to pray. I used to do all my reciting with her, for Mother's Day, Easter, Christmas, all the holidays at the church. She'd say, "Don't singsong, Kate, don't singsong." I'd go in and recite and she'd say, "Now slow down and say it like this . . ." She was an artist in that sense, she really believed in poetry. She read *Guideposts* religiously, *Ideal Magazine*, and *Reader's Digest Condensed Books*. She had this long prayer that she'd pray after all the food was on the table. We always knew she was getting to the end when she said, "And when waste and age and shock and strife shall have sapped these walls of life, take this dust of earthly worn and mold it into heavenly form."

She was a very religious woman and she didn't believe in anger. She'd say, "It's nice to be important but more important to be nice." Christianity and niceness were synonymous for her, so she got pushed around a lot and exploited a lot. We couldn't laugh at anybody, never poke fun at any kid. There was a man in our neighborhood who looked like the elephant man with warts all over him. All the kids would run from him. She'd sit us down and say, "God made everybody." Sometimes kids would be poking fun at other kids because they had raggedy clothes and raggedy shoes, and she'd say, "No, you don't do that." I'd feel so cheated because I couldn't be like a normal kid, that I had to be this damn Christian all the time. But I'm so glad she gave us that, because even when the tables were turned and I was the poor one and the raggedy one, I still knew I was somebody.

My grandmother gave us a sense of stability. When she died, the hardest thing was calling home and realizing nobody was home. As long as she was alive, there was always someone home.

Our house changed over the years. What I first remember is that you walked in the front door and that was my parents' bedroom and there was always a baby crib in there. To the left was the dining room with an oil stove and a buffet and a china cabinet. Then there was a kitchen and another bedroom. There were nine of us and we kids slept in the back room. All the rooms were painted green. Our house expanded over the years and another bedroom and a bathroom were added on eventually. When I was growing up we had an outhouse out back. Our yard had a garden, pear trees, a plum tree, apple trees, cherry trees, muscadine, a grapevine, and a big holler in the back where we dumped our garbage and burned it. The holler led all the way back to the hog pen, the smoke house, and a coal house, a garage and a chicken coop. The front yard had hedges all around, grass, and a walkway. The back yard didn't have grass so we swept it and kept it nice and clean. We had a clothes line out there. One of the ways we knew we were upwardly mobile is when we moved the clothes line so that you couldn't see the underwear from the road.

My mother's name is Corrine Emmanuelette Lytle Cannon. She

was named for her father Emmanuel. She was the nineteenth child of twenty. She loved her mother. Grandma died in her arms. She always wanted to be a schoolteacher or a businesswoman. She had so many dreams. When she realized that she couldn't fulfill her dreams, she just gave those dreams to us. Most people think she is a teacher or something because of the way she carries herself, proud-like, a real survivor. If there was an opportunity to go somewhere for the church, "I'll go, I'll go do it." So some of the older schoolteachers and people in the church exposed her to things that normally one without an education would not get exposed to. She wanted to go to business college, and we had one of those real old typewriters in our house.

She is a very shapely woman and dresses very well. The house was hers and she let us know that. Her husband was hers too and she let us know that. I never knew my father because he was off limits to us. That was her man. "He's mine, get your own man," she'd say. We were appendages to their marriage, we could never come between them. That's probably why they have been so happily married for forty-five years. I never knew my mother to take a bath without my father washing her back. He'd be out in the yard, and she'd say, "Go get your daddy. Esau, come here." And he'd always come. She had him wrapped around her little finger.

My mother took us everywhere. Most black kids stayed at home, but we'd get dressed up and we'd go. We got exposed to Jim Crowism because we were always going out. And of course Mama would say, "Go to the bathroom before we leave. . . . Eat before we leave," because we couldn't do either until we got back. She almost jerked my arm off one time because I saw one of the white women she cleaned for and said, "Mama, there's Mrs. Coates." You didn't talk to those people in the streets. Mama was always clean and dressed up with her hair done. She wasn't going to stop going because of us, and she'd be damned if we were going to hold her up being children. So we learned manners early on, how to act in public, how to speak up, how to talk, and how not to make demands. We'd go with her when she went shopping and when she went to the doctor's. She'd have to go up the back stairs and we'd learn to sit in the car for three or four hours without fighting or anything. You took a book to read and acted mannerly. There was a lot of control. When I was already in school and knew about gym sets and swings, we parked in front of the Presbyterian Church in Charlotte and I wanted to go play on the swings in the playground. She told me, "Kate, you can't do that." My experience was that my mother exposed me to the world as it was without protection, and she also taught us how to cope with it, so we all learned our place.

My mother worked as a domestic. At one point she made five dollars a week, and then she found by working for different people she could make five dollars a day. My mother also did all these little odd jobs like sell Stanley Products, vanilla flavoring and liniment, and collect burial money. She did all those things to keep us in kindergarten, and she always tithed. She taught us to give ten percent to the church that we went to every Sunday. Every Sunday. We went to the Presbyterian church and she always had to pick up every kid in the neighborhood. There was never any private space. We were always crowded in our 1957 Chevy station wagon. "Well, you know, they got to go to church too," she'd say.

It was always assumed that we would work. Work was a given in life, almost like breathing and sleeping. I'm always surprised when I hear people talking about somebody taking care of them, because we always knew we were going to work. The first work I did was as a domestic, cleaning people's houses. The interesting thing was that all the white people we worked for were mill workers. Black women were not allowed to work in the mill then, so the only jobs available to black women were as domestics or teachers, and there was only one black school in Kannapolis. They only needed about thirty teachers, so that was very limited. All the black women I knew worked as domestics and all the black men I knew worked in Cannon Mills in the low-paying menial jobs. My father drove a truck and did whatever dirty work there was to be done. As I said, my grandmother's greatest pride was that she never worked for a white person, and she used to ridicule my mother in a very covert, subtle way for not having a better job. I was never ashamed that my mother was a domestic because everybody else's mother was a domestic, if they worked at all. So I knew I'd grow up to be a domestic.

Part of the training for black kids to become a domestic was to learn to do that kind of work at home. 'Cause while your mother's taking care of white kids and cleaning up white houses, you got to do that for yourself. There is nothing that would irritate a black woman more than to clean a white woman's house all day long and then come home to a dirty house. In some kind of way, almost as if by osmosis, black girls were supposed to know how to do all these things and who was supposed to be teaching us? Mama would leave before sunup and when she got home it would be sundown, and we were not only supposed to know how to keep house but also how to cook perfect meals and not burn food up, and not to eat up all the food because it had to stretch. This wisdom was supposed to be inside of each of us, I mean, we were disciplined if we didn't know it. So that was very frustrating. That's how I learned to be a domestic, by taking care of house at home. My older sister, who was two years older than me, was responsible for teaching me how to do it. How to mop the floors, how to pick the strings up after the mop, how to dust so that you don't break things, how to wash windows and wipe down the blinds, the whole mechanical system of how to clean a house. I knew all that by the time I was eight. If you didn't do it right you got screamed at. You just figured it out so you wouldn't get hit. It was like, "How did you miss this?" And "Why is there a streak here?" "What are these strings doing on the floor?" Or "You missed this corner." It was like a spot check when she got home, especially on Saturdays, because that was when we were supposed to really clean house and get our clothes ready for Sunday.

So I started working for my aunt who cleaned the house down the road and got two dollars for the day. That was my very first job. I was so proud of it too, 'cause that meant that I had learned at home how to do it. Aunt Tot has always drank a lot, has all

Amazon mill village, 1984. Photo by the author.

her life, but she always liked me. Whenever she didn't want to go to work she'd let different nieces take over. Well, I was so honored that she'd let me work for her as a domestic. She said, "Kate, you want to make some money?" It was two dollars and in 1962 that was like a lot of money. She told me it was for the Chapmans down the road. She told me to go down there and she didn't have to tell me what to do specifically, she just told me to put the dinner on, that I had to cook, wash the clothes, iron the clothes, take care of the children and make sure nothing happens to them. Most of the time they didn't want you to wash the floors with a mop, they wanted you to get down on your hands and knees and wash all the corners and stuff.

I was told not to do anything that would cause Aunt Tot to lose her job. So I was meticulous in everything I did because— one, I wanted my aunt to be proud of me, and two, my mother's reputation was on the line because she was training me to be a domestic, and three, my aunt's income was on the line because if anything was broken or not up to par then she could lose her job. The fact that she was going to give me the whole two dollars was a real honor. So I'd walk down to Mrs. Chapman's house and clean up her house and take care of her four kids. One of the daughters was as old as I was, maybe twelve, named Blondie. They would sit around and watch TV and play games, and they didn't think anything of the fact that I was cleaning. I was just Tot's niece who would come in whenever she wasn't there. Aunt Tot was probably out drinking or something but I felt real glad that she would let me come in and do it. That was my first job where I got paid. Mrs. Chapman worked in the mill and so did her husband. He would be there when I got there, and he'd just be leaving. She worked first shift and he worked second. In Kannapolis you can't get through the center of town during the changing of shifts, it's so jammed.

I remember their house was tinier than ours, and there were things in their house that were not even as nice as ours. Most of the white people in Kannapolis didn't clean their houses. That was what black women were for. That was how black women would get their income, how they survived. So the Chapmans had this old house, it was like four rooms. Our house was small but larger than the house they lived in.

They would pay you two dollars for two hours of work, but you had a list of things to do and if it took you longer than that, that was your business. All the work they wanted you to do, you could never do in two hours. You had to wash the clothes, hang them on the line and iron them, wash the floors, and do things like clean the refrigerator or clean out the cabinets, all these other little things you did to prove you were worthy of the job. You never did just what you were asked. You always did a little extra. I remember you never ate the food. That was just not a sign of a good domestic. They had food like baloney, which was considered white people's food anyway, so you brought your own food. I'd bring potted meat, sardines, or vienna sausages.

I resented those Chapman kids. I resented the fact that my mother was always gone and didn't have time to take care of her kids and here I was a kid having to take care of kids who were my same age.

BORN A WOMANCHILD

In North Carolina, South Carolina, Georgia, and Alabama, the New South's industrialization began to form upon the foundation of the textile industry. The concurrent development of the tobacco industry provided additional capital for hydroelectric power which was to run the mills. A dramatic increase in southern rail mileage, from eight thousand miles to more than twenty thousand, helped to decentralize manufacturing and textiles in the South. Also the ring spindle* and the automatic loom rendered skilled labor unnecessary. These factors paved the way for southern mill owners to open their doors to the greatest economic advantage the South had over the North—an abundance of cheap and willing labor. The industry's growth was based on a vastly expanding number of women and children in the mills. In the four textile states in 1890, men formed only 35 percent of the work force, women made up 40 percent, and children between the ages of ten and fifteen made up 25 percent. A seventy-hour workweek earned about $2.50 in 1885 and slightly less in 1895. At the same time profits were phenomenal. According to his-

*A ring spindle is a spinning machine
in which the thread passes through a
metal loop and then revolves around
each spindle.

torian Broadus Mitchell, "It was not unusual . . . in these years to make 30 to 70 percent profit."*

This large southern work force, reportedly eager to put in their eleven- to twelve-hour workday, quickly caught the attention of New England mill owners, who were by then well-established entrepreneurs aggravated by the North's newly formed textile unions. Gradually northern businessmen began to divert capital to the South. Southern labor, it was reported, was in no way union-minded nor wise to the ways of organization.

Lower wages and longer hours accounted for cheaper cotton manufacturing in the South. Southern states permitted night work for women, and the eleven-hour workday six days a week and twelve-hour worknight five nights a week were common. In the South, children of fourteen could, by law, work the same hours as adults, but at the Amazon mill, children started to work at a much younger age.

Because of the pressures and demands of large families, poor and working-class southern girls of the early twentieth century assumed the responsibilities of adulthood at a tender age. Their labor power was needed, whether in the cotton field or the cotton mill, for the economic survival of their families. In white families, girls often worked alongside their parents and brothers in the fields, and were also responsible for domestic chores and child-rearing. When the transition from farm to factory was made in the early part of this century, white girls as young as seven found employment in the mills. Their wages were considered a part of household funds and used for buying food and clothes for the family. These children, who might have worked a sixty-four-hour workweek, were allowed to keep maybe twenty-five cents of their wages, if any, after household expenses were taken care of. Many children looked forward to becoming of age to work in the mill as a way of getting out of the hot and back-breaking work of farming, while others would have preferred to remain on the farm.

*Mitchell, Broadus. *The Rise of the
Cotton Mills in the South.* Baltimore:
Johns Hopkins Press, 1921.

The choice, however, was not theirs to make. If it had been, all the women I talked to would have chosen to be in school.

In black families, girls were put in the fields as soon as they were able to hoe or pick cotton, usually around age five. They did not have the alternative of mill work like their white counterparts. Therefore, most black girls spent their childhoods in the fields until around age twelve, when they were hired out as domestics and lived in the homes of white families, where they were responsible for housework, cooking, and child care.

The working-class southern girl of the early twentieth century was born in severe poverty and raised without protection. She survived overcrowded living conditions, poor nutrition and in some cases starvation, little if any education, an often hostile and violent environment, and a life overwhelmingly centered around work. Only in the first years of life and, later, perhaps for a few hours on Sunday, was there time for these children to play.

BERTHA MILLER

Thomasville, North Carolina

I was born in Randolph County ninety years ago. I wanted to be a farmer. Yeah, but I didn't get to be one. I was raised on a farm and I like a farm. I'd rather plow than do any other kind of work I've ever done in my life. We rented our land, we didn't own it, but we had all we wanted to tend. We raised corn, wheat, barley, tobacco, and enough cotton to make quilts and stuff like that. That was the best living I ever did, was living on a farm. We'd go possum hunting, rabbit hunting, cut wood together, work on the farm, and me and my daddy, we'd plow. I remember old Doc Phillips come walking by one day. Doc Phillips brought me in this world and all my younguns too. We lived side by side down in the country. So that day he come walking by and I was plowing corn. He stopped there at the house and hollered for me to come in the house. He said, "You're going to get killed on that thing." And I said, "No I ain't. I reckon I got enough sense to plow." I wasn't nothing but a youngun then.

My grandpap used to live with us. He made coffins. He lived with us for years, then he went back to his little home in the country and that's where he died. My daddy, he was a hard worker. I remember he got sick after we come to town. He worked down at the cotton mill for several years until he got down, plumb down, and wanted to go back home to the farm. That's where he died. My mother was a little old bitty thing, weighed about ninety pounds. She was a good Christian woman. When we moved

Bertha Miller, *right,* with a friend, about 1915.
Photo courtesy of Bertha Miller.

here from the country, she went out there at the cotton mill and went to work. We all did.

I was so little for my age that at three years old, old Doc Phillips told my mother, he said, "Lou, give Pug,"—he always called me Pug—"a chew of tobacco." That was going to make me grow. So Ma cut me off a little chew of tobacco and I just chomped on it. First thing I knew my head started going around maybe ninety miles an hour and oh I was sick. I just laid down on the porch and vomited like a dog. I thought I was going to vomit my insides out. But I kept tasting it along and finally one day I said, "Give me a dip of snuff, maybe it won't make me sick." But it did. Still I kept dipping it a little longer 'til I got to where I dipped it regular. Then I started to grow. When I worked in the mill, just about all the girls in there dipped snuff. They dipped to keep the lint out of their throats. You never saw a woman smoking cigarettes back then. The awfullest looking sight I ever saw was a woman smoking a cigarette. I thought, Lord help.

I was eleven years old when I went to work in the mill. They learnt me to knit. Well, I was so little that they had to build me a box to get up on to put the sock in the machine. I worked in the hosiery mill for a long time and, well, then we moved back to the country. But me and my sister Molly finally went back up there in 1910 and I went to work in the silk mill. Molly went to work in the hosiery mill. I come over here in 1912 and boarded with Green Davis and Lou. They kept four other mill girls besides me. We all worked in the Amazon Cotton Mill. When we weren't working in the mill, there wasn't nothing much to do only sit around there and laugh and talk. Us girls, we'd wash our clothes and stuff like that. That's all there was to do. There weren't no place to go. We'd go to the show every once in a while, but it was so far to walk to town. Still, we had a good time. Mrs. Welch lived beside of us and she had three girls. We'd all get together and sing and go on. Me, Berthie, Nan, and all of us, we'd get in one room and we'd sing religious songs and laugh and talk. We'd have a good time and enjoyed ourselves right there in the house. Weren't allowed to go nowhere. Didn't get out and frolic around

Bertha Miller, 1984.
Photo by the author.

at night. We'd just sit right there at home and talk about what we was going to do when we got old enough to get married and all such things as that. We worked twelve hours a day for fifty cents. When paydays come around, I drawed three dollars. That was for six days a week, seventy-two hours. I remember I lacked fifty cents having enough to pay my board.

MARGARET CAUTHEN

Kannapolis, North Carolina

I was born April 11, 1934, in a little place called Ludus-town, and we were the only black folks there. Then we moved back to Davidson County and lived there in the country for nineteen years. Then my daddy sold the farm and as each one of us graduated from high school, we all got jobs. Then we moved over here to Kannapolis and we been over here for twenty-six years. Our farm was more of an orchard. We grew fruit and we had to pick it and grade it. Daddy worked at Cabarrus Hospital as an aide. At cotton picking time, we would go to my grandmother's house and help them pick their cotton. We had no cotton on our farm. But we had all kinds of fruit and we had a garden where we raised our food. We raised hogs, had a cow and an old mule. There were seven of us kids, three boys and four girls. I was the middle child. Mama stayed with us when we was small and then she did domestic work.

I was around six or seven, something like that, when I first went to work in the cotton field. We'd go up there to my grandmother's house and stay during the week and come home on the weekends. We'd get up early, at the break of day, and go downstairs and eat breakfast. Then we'd go to the fields and we'd be standing there talkin' and we might have to go to the bathroom. You know, out in the woods. Then we'd go to work. Mama would be with us.

We wore pants and a shirt and a hat, and was it hot! Ooh, it be hot! We be picking cotton and in some places the cotton be tall and we be sitting on our sack under that tall cotton in the shade until Mama spied us and then she'd holler at us, and we'd say, "Oh, we'll pick it." Or we'd be saying we have to go pee-pee and we'd run in the wood and hide in the shade until Mama would come and she'd squall for us to come out. At the end of the day, they would weigh up the cotton, weigh it up to see how much you had. Well, my oldest sister, she never was a cotton picker, I could pick more than her, so we'd get water, drinking water, and we'd pour it in the cotton bag to make it heavy so it would weigh more. You'd take dry cotton and put it over that wet cotton at the bottom. So this particular day she thought she would put a rock in her basket. Sometimes we used to have baskets and they would weigh your cotton and subtract the weight of the basket. So this day she put a rock in her basket and they found that rock and when they did she said I did it and I was the one that got the whipping. We didn't have a certain amount to pick, you just did the best you could. But you were expected to pick at least fifty pounds of cotton. That was a lot of cotton, and it took all day. You had a sack and if it wasn't full then they would know you hadn't done anything, so we would get a whipping at the end of the day. But when it came time to come home, whether we were going to get a whipping or not, we be glad to come home.

I grew up in a big old wooden house that had four rooms with a big front room and a big old hall. There was only one house up on a hill that we could see from our house and there was woods that separated us from our neighbors. As kids we played hopscotch, softball, horseshoes, jump the rope, kick the can, and crack the whip. And, oh Lord yes, we played dolls and made doll houses. We had a holler and in that holler was red clay, so we'd get buckets and go get it and bring it to the house. Then we'd make our dolls furniture and see, we'd sit it out in the sun and it would get hard, it wouldn't break. We'd make clay doll houses and we'd put this furniture in it. Then we'd take catalogues and cut it out for people. Then we'd play cooking and we'd get these great big old green leaves and put them in a can and build a fire.

Mama wouldn't be there. And we'd cook that stuff and it would stink. Then we'd try to make the dog eat it. Then we'd play with the cats and dress them up like our babies and they'd scratch us and we'd take the chickens and play like they were our babies and the old hen would come and jump on us. We used to do some terrible things for fun.

My mama was a good mama and she loved to can. She had a sister, Aunt Bert, who lived in Philadelphia, and she would come down every summer. Mama had seven children and so did she. They'd come every summer from the time strawberries start berrying. That be in May. Okay, Aunt Bert would come and we kids would sleep on pallets. Mama would get up early that morning, her and Aunt Bert. They'd go pick the berries and we'd have to go down and get water from the spring and clean up all the jars. So they'd get back from berrying and sometimes they'd let the oldest ones cap, which is taking off the hull and stem, but they wouldn't let the younguns because we would squash 'em. We would have to carry all the water for washing the berries and cooking them and then canning them. So Aunt Bert would stay the whole summer and the whole time she'd be standing there canning. We be carrying water, washing the fruits, the apples or peaches or whatever we was canning. So we'd be toting water and hauling out the peach peels or whatever and taking them down to the hogs. They'd be canning jellies or anything that would go in a jar, that's what they canned. And Mama had what she called a pantry and she'd put all that stuff in there and it be filled from top to bottom.

Then we'd go cressie green hunting in the morning and come back at lunch time and set up some cressie greens.* We'd have to wash them things over and over and over again.

Now at hog time the neighbors would come. If you knew someone was going to kill hogs, you'd go help them and then they'd come and help you. We didn't see any of that. Mama

---

* Cressies are tender, edible greens
similar to collards.

wouldn't let us. We carried water from the spring to clean the meat, but we didn't do too much around the hogs.

I was close to my mama. We was always sitting and talking while we worked. She'd tell me about coming up. She only had two brothers and back then the girls had to do the same as the men would do on the farm. There was ten younguns all together in her family and only two boys, so the girls had to do the plowing just like the men. I tried to do some plowing but I plowed too deep in the ground. There's a certain way you got to hold that plow because if you don't it will go deep, deep down in the ground and that's what happened when I tried so I couldn't do that. We carried fertilizer for the fertilizer distributor and we carried water when Daddy put out plants. My mama was religious, so every Sunday morning we'd be in Sunday school. Well, we'd be in church all day. Oh yeah, we would be in church *every* Sunday. We're Methodist Zion and we did everything that the church did.

MARY LEE BOST

Kannapolis, North Carolina

I was born in 1923 in Cabbarus County on the Rankin Farm. Frank Rankin's farm. We worked the crops on the Rankin Farm, you know, cotton. Sharecroppin'. I didn't stay with my mother then. My grandmother raised me. I was born in her house and so they just kept me. My grandmother and my grandfather raised me from a baby and I stayed with them until I got up old enough to work out in the public. I was raised up with my grandmother's children, five girls and four boys. We was all raised up together. They was all like sisters and brothers to me. I never did call any one of them uncle or aunt. And most everybody thought I was their sister because we looked so much alike. We'd play hopscotch, ring around the roses, you didn't have so many toys back then. I had a rockin' chair that Santie Claus had brought me, and I wouldn't let nobody sit in that chair. I learned to hide that chair. When my baby sister would come to see us I wouldn't let her sit in that chair, because it was mine. But my grandmother would say, "Now, let her sit in it," and I'd say, "Well, I'll let her sit in it if she don't break it."

I was about five or six when I started going to the field to pick cotton. I'd run along and pick cotton and put it in my grandmother's bag, and slip and throw cotton balls and run and hide. My grandmother, when she would get ready to go to the cotton fields—she'd have a big old wood stove and big old iron pots—maybe she'd have a big old pot of pinto beans on, a big pot of cabbage, maybe Irish potatoes, and she'd sit 'em on the back of

55

the stove and then about eleven o'clock she'd always come up and make biscuits and have dinner ready when the others would come up. Then after we'd get through eating, we'd take a break and lay under the shade tree. If it was real hot we'd lay somewhere it was cool, you know.

When I got big enough where I could do something, I was sick all the time, because I didn't like to hoe cotton when it was so hot. Instead of being hoeing I'd be leaning on my hoe looking at the sun and it be so hot. Then my grandmother would say, "Get on off the hoe and start hoeing cotton." Said, "You ain't gonna get through like that." So I'd go on and dinner time would come and I'd have one of the awfulest headaches. And my grandfather would say, "Oh, don't make her go back to the field, she's got a headache." And Mama would say, "Ain't a thing wrong with her only she don't want to go and hoe cotton," and there wouldn't be a thing wrong with me. But I'd get to stay home. I'd be playing, laying out there by the shed. There used to be a big old oak tree and I'd play underneath it in the shade with what we called doodle holes. I'd get out there and say, "Come on doodle, come and get some butter and bread." And you'd see the sand just a workin', and they'd come up too. Then I'd say, "Back up doodle," and they'd back up. Doodles were like little black bugs, but they would, they'd come up. Then as they come up out of the ground, I'd say, "Back back, doodle," and they'd back back.

I remember one time in the summertime we was staying on Mooresville Road, and all of 'em was stripping lassey cane, what you make molasses out of, and so I always had to go and get the cow. I'd have to go and bring her up to get some water. And this time I don't know what happened to her but she didn't want to be messed with. So she started running and I was running trying to catch the chain, you know, and my foot got caught in it. And she started running and she dragged me I don't know how far. Well, it just happened that my uncle had come up with the mules to give them some water and he heard me hollerin', "Oh Lordy, somebody help me!" So he came running and this cow was headed down toward the swamp and she was just draggin' me. So he got her stopped and got me untangled. He stood me up, and said, "Lord, Mary Lee, just look at the blood running down your leg." And I looked down and I started crying. So he carried me on up to the house. We had a bell and we'd ring it when something like this happened so everybody would know and come on back to the house. So this lady and her son was helping my grandfather strip lassey cane. So we could see 'em; they was coming; running up from the field. So all this skin on my legs and back was gone. So this lady told my mama that she had some powder and she told her son to go and get it. She said to beat it up, kinda parch it and put it all on that place. She said it gonna be burning and when they did, oh Lord have mercy, I hollered and cried. My grandfather got so mad at that cow that he went and got his shotgun and shot that cow. He didn't kill it; shot it in the hip and the next week he sold it. So I couldn't hardly put no clothes on because I was all skinned up. My grandmother had to pin a diaper on me. And I couldn't sit down, I had to lay down on my stomach.

So that night Daddy carried me upstairs and put me to bed. And when I woke up the next morning that sheet had all just stuck to me. So my grandmother had to take the scissors and cut that sheet from around me. So they carried me from the bed and brought me down and laid me down on the bench. Back then they had that lye soap that had that awful smell and so she mixed it with water and made suds and put those suds on me and let it dry. Then the sheet came off and she kept using that soap until a scab got on it. So one morning I was standing in the door and my aunt had to wash the dishes that morning. You know we all had chores to do, but she was mad that she had to wash dishes that morning and she pushed me out the door. Well, I slipped and fell and knocked that great big scab off. So it was raw again. But Mama used soap suds on it until it finally healed up. I was about ten years old then.

See, people didn't use doctors back then like they do now. No, they sure didn't. Now, when I got a cold, my grandmother always used those old-time remedies. She made up her brews and stuff.

She'd make horehound tea and all that stuff. Then she'd make up some homemade grease from the tallow that comes from goat. It's white looking and kindly hard and she would cut it with a knife just like soap or something. It comes from the goat's fat. So she would make up grease. Back then we had fireplaces and we'd have on long flannel gowns. We'd get that grease at night before we'd go to bed, and we'd grease our feets and grease our chests in front of the fire. She'd get us as greasy as she could get and she'd take a brown paper bag and grease that paper bag and we'd sit there and get it hot and then we'd go to bed and she'd pin that paper bag to us. The next morning that cold be done broke.

She always had some remedy. She used to be bothered by asthma and she would go to the woods and get these pine needles off the tree and make her a pillow out of these pine needles. She'd sleep on it until those needles started getting dry. Then she'd take them out and put more pine needles in there. Then she wouldn't be bothered with asthma no more. Now for a stomach-ache she used to use what she called camel's root. You'd get the root part and wash it. Camel root looks like the long leafy part of a gladiola. I got some growing out there now. And you'd wash the root part and chew it and swallow the juice and it would get rid of a stomachache. I just sent some of that camel's root to my first cousin. She wrote me and wanted to know if anybody had any camel's root. I grow it out there in the front yard.

Mama was also a midwife. We lived over there near the McKinleys. When their children would get sick, they'd get grav-els, you know, how little children would eat rocks and things and it would get stuck in their bowels and she would go up there and work on them. Everybody called her Aunt Daisy. You know, babies, when they eyes would water, my grandmother would always get catnip leaves and wash them real good and boil them. Then she'd take the leaves out and put that water in the bottle and give it to them. She always had a cure. She would get seeds from people or sprouts, like catnip sprouts, and she would grow these things around the house. Then when women got ready to have their babies, she'd go out and deliver them. Sometimes people would give her some kind of payment for her work and then sometimes if a child was sick, she would go do the best she could do and not take nothing for it. I guess the Lord just blessed her like that. Finally, she had to give it up because the doctors come in and they cut out the midwife. She was ninety-nine years old when she died. She was a real nice looking lady. She had high cheekbones and she never used no curse words or anything like that.

Right before she died, she had bad circulation and she had a sore toe that wouldn't heal because of that bad circulation. So I'd come in every morning on my way to work to see her and when she'd wake up the first thing she'd say is, "Is Mary Lee here yet?" So I'd come in and I'd say, "Mama," and she'd say, "Is that you, Mary Lee? Will you come in here and bathe my toe for me? It hurts so bad." So I'd say yes. I'd go get the water and the stuff to put in it and bathe her foot for her, then I'd wrap it back up and everything and then she'd say, "Seems like that just helps it so much." See, she wanted me to do it, and if anybody else had already bathed her foot, she'd ask me to do it again for her.

I called my grandmother Mama and I called my real mother by her name, 'cause my grandmother raised me. When my real mother came around they wouldn't make me call her Mama. So I called her what everybody else did. I just called her Irene. It kindly felt like my real mother was my sister because, see, she didn't raise me and my grandmother felt like my real mama, and all my grandmother's children felt like my sisters and brothers. So I just called her Mama. Everybody would say that's your mama and I'd say I know it is, but I just couldn't ever get my mouth to say Mama. She had had me when she was real young before she was married but I lived there and it all felt like my sisters and brothers, like family. She would come to see me but she got married and lived down in the country. I made up my mind one time that I was going to go live with my real mama and my baby sisters. So my grandmother packed my little bag, you know, and she told Irene, my real mother, "No, she's not going to go home with you, she's going to wait until you get almost home and then she's going to start crying." So I went out there and sat down beside my mother and my sisters in our old car and we were off, but just as they turned into the driveway, I busted out crying. So they had to send me back home.

I stayed in school until I got up big enough to help my grandmother some. Then I quit school and I went to work. The first job I got I worked up here and stayed on the lot and made three dollars a week. I wasn't cooking, I was just helping the lady clean up. I was probably about fifteen or sixteen, something like that. Back then if you had three dollars you thought you had something. I used that money to help buy groceries for my grandmother and grandfather when the crops didn't do so good. The next week I'd buy me a pair of shoes. Lord, I just thought I was rich. This was about 1938. Then I went to cooking and I lived on the lot cleaning and watching kids for these white women that worked in the mill. I'd go home on the weekends. I would see my father on the weekends. He would come by and pick me up and take me over to my grandmother's. He drove an old T-Model.

I'd get these jobs from somebody telling them about me. They'd say well Mary Lee so-and-so. They had to know you somehow so they could trust you, 'cause a lot of them said their maids would steal things, you know. My grandmother always told me don't never take nothing that don't belong to you. What you don't need, don't never throw it away, give it to someone who needs it. And always try to do the best you can. Do the best you can and that's all you can do. And I always tried to do the best I could do. I could go out here and work three houses a day if I was able, because so many people wanted me to work for them.

When I was little it didn't even cross my mind what I wanted to be, just as long as I had my room and board. My family was poorer than most others but we survived and we got along. I always wanted to cook when I was little and so my grandmother would give me a little bit of flour and let me make up something. But she would always make me eat my own cooking, so I learned to cook. Ask around about my egg custards and my Sundrop cakes. I can cook, now I ain't bragging, but I can cook.

BERTHA AWFORD BLACK

Thomasville, North Carolina

I've been living right here on Trotter Street for seventy years. I was the seventh child, born March 5, 1899. My grandfather was a minister of the Christian faith. He was a riding evangelist. My grandmother died when my mother was about four years old and my grandfather raised her. He would put her on that horse and ride her with him, you know. He was a circuit rider they called it. He went from church to church, wherever he was called to preach. He made his living that way and farming. They lived down near Ashboro. Then when my mother got married, they moved to Trinity. We lived there until I was eleven, and then we moved here and we been living here ever since. We moved here so we could all go to work in the mill.

When we lived in Trinity, we farmed all kinds of vegetables, wheat, and just a little cotton. My mama and daddy had twenty-one acres of clearin' and then rented some more land. I reckon one day they took a notion to leave out and make some money. They couldn't get nothing out of raising vegetables. We were living in a log house on the farm. It was a three-room house and the floor was laid with wide planks. I remember them planks because they was always loose. That was the house where I was born, and there was twelve of us all together, my mama and daddy and ten children. The house had an upstairs and a downstairs, and the boys, they slept upstairs, and the girls downstairs. Four beds in a room. All us kids was born about two years apart, and when we moved to town every one of us younguns went to work in the mill. That was in the early winter of 1911. My daddy went back and forth from the farm selling vegetables for a while and then he finally went to work. We all went to work in the Amazon Cotton Mill and we all worked there all our lives.

My mother was a good giver of orders. She had to be to look after that crowd. There was five girls and five boys. We girls had to clean house, cook, do laundry, and I mean you had to do it in a wash tub with a scrub board. We would wash all day long. The boys did the outside chores. They cut the wood and stuff like that. When we lived in Trinity we had to carry water from here to that store out yonder. Now that's the truth. Both the boys and the girls carried water. We had to carry water enough to do all that laundry.

My father was a happy-go-lucky fellow. He never saw nothing that a child did that deserved a spanking. Now Mama would spank us, and when she did my daddy would say, "Just kill him, just cut his head off." Just foolin', but now I'll tell you, ain't like children is this day and time. If we was up in the woods and our mother or daddy would call us from the house, we didn't say "Wait a minute." They didn't abuse us either, but when they called us we went on and done what they said to do. That's the way we growed up, that's the way they teached us to be.

When we moved to Thomasville, we lived over there right in front of the old drugstore beside the cotton mill. We lived in a cotton mill house there, and then we moved down to another mill house on Concord Street. That one is still there. It was a new house then—they had just built it. It had plaster walls and we moved into a four-room house. The mill had three-room and four-room houses, so we moved into a four-room house. I was eleven and my sister was ten when we went to work in the mill. The girl that trained me was younger than that. I stayed with her, her a-learnin' me, for about two weeks, and I didn't get nothing for it. Not while I was a-learnin'. Then they put me on two sides, two spinning frames, and I made twenty-five cents a day. We went in at six in the morning and got out at six at night.

Bertha Black.
Photo by the author.

And we worked Saturday when we first come here, from six in the morning to four in the evening. I worked two weeks and my first payday I drawed $2.50. I know that just as good as if it happened yesterday. I thought I had some money! After a few weeks' time I got to where I could run six sides. That was seventy-five cents a day and I drawed nine dollars for a full payday every two weeks. I'd take that money and I'd give it to our mother. We all did, because she raised the family, bought our food and clothes. She always looked after us good. I mean, we dressed as good as the rest of 'em. Back then for a dollar or two you could dress yourself up pretty nice. A dollar for a dress and ninety-eight cents for a pair of shoes. For five dollars you could really do it up with a hat and a handbag. We'd buy our clothes already made at Kresses and then there was a general store and Mother had credit there. Sometimes my sister, my oldest sister, would make our dresses. She'd buy cloth for five cents and lace for a penny. So she'd make us a dress for maybe a quarter. But mostly we had to buy what we had 'cause we worked in the mill and didn't have a whole lot of time for sewin'.

We were all anxious to go to work because, I don't know, we didn't like the farming. It was so hot and from sunup to sundown. No, that was not for me. Mill work was better. It had to be. Once we went to work in the mill after we moved here from the farm, we had more clothes and more different kinds of food than we did when we was a-farmin'. And we had a better house. They kept them mill houses up pretty good at first. That house we had farming, at first it was just a log house. Then my daddy weatherproofed it and sealed it. It had a fireplace in it, a great big fireplace, and we'd throw a long log in it, so it was a warm house. Then he built a living room onto it, but you'd have to go outside and across the back porch to get to the kitchen. So we had a better house in the mill village, better clothes, and better food. We kept a vegetable garden right here in Thomasville. We'd have hogs and a cow and we wouldn't have to buy anything from the grocery store in the way of meat. When we lived in Trinity, we'd buy beef from a man who came around in a covered wagon, a man selling fresh beef, and Mama would cook it in a big iron pot that hung over the fire in the fireplace. Then she had a skillet, a great big old thing with a lid on it that stood on three iron legs. She could bake bread and sweet potatoes in that thing right there in the fireplace. So yes, when we came to the mill life was easier.

My first day in the mill, I was scared, yeah, like a kid would be. I didn't know what they did in there. The biggest portion of the spinners was kids back then. We'd piece up sometimes after the doffing boys who doffed the frames and we'd get caught up.* Well, we'd go out there behind the mill at the warehouse and us girls we'd build us a little playhouse until they'd whistle for us and yell, "Time for the doffers to piece up again." Just nothing but children. You know, that ought to have been stopped a long time before it was. We didn't get no education. We weren't old enough to go to work. That thar child labor law was wonderful when it came in. We, every one, should have been in school.

* In spinning, when the cotton being spun breaks, the two ends are tied together, or pieced up. A doffer is a worker who removes the spools filled by the spinning machine.

GEORGIANNA NOVELLA HUNT

Kannapolis, North Carolina

I was born out of wedlock. My mama and daddy wasn't married. I don't know, my mama said I was born in 1907, the twenty-sixth of February, and that's what I been keepin' up with. A schoolteacher used to live right over there—she died since I been gone—she wrote it down because I don't think they was givin' birth certificates when I was born. But anyway, she had wrote a letter tellin' where I was born at and all that and found out. But I really don't know when I was born. That's what Mama told me, February 26, 1907, and that's what I been keepin' up—child, I'm old. I ain't got a black hair in my head. But I just put on a hat or something and go on.

So many different peoples raised me I really don't know who to say raised me. I'm just tellin' you the truth. So many peoples I can't even remember. I can't even get around down here. When I first came back I had a car and I couldn't get around in Concord. I was scared I be looking at the numbers and I might run over somebody. Things has changed so much. Everything looks strange to me since I been back. I was really small when I left, I reckon I was around about twelve or thirteen. I'm gonna tell you the truth, I really don't know the first place I went. We was livin' over there in the country, me and Mama, over there in the country, and when I left I went over there to Tin Cup over there in Kannapolis. I walked from over there to Tip Cup. Tin Cup was a little place back there over town, I can't even find it now. Somewhere down there in the holler. Tin Cup was just like Fisher

Town but over in Kannapolis. It was like that. I asked several people since I been here and they try to tell me where's it at. I can't find it. I went to live there with my Aunt Bertha and Uncle John.

I don't know how long I stayed there. Really I don't know. No suh. The reason I went to live there was see, I had a stepfather and he tried to have his way with me.

We was fishin' in a lake. I was on one side and he was on the other and I kept a feelin' him lookin' at me. But I was young and I didn't know. At last he rolled up his hook and come over there where I was. He stood there and looked at me and said "Georgiana." I said "Yes suh." He said "Your little bubbles growing mighty fast." He said "I know you let the little boys tickle 'em, why not let me?" And I got right up and said "I'm going to tell my mama." And I lit out to come to home and he lit out in front of me and beat me to the house. So I was scared to tell mama then. But I told her the next day. So I left because he beat me and told me to go. It was raining and I was hurtin' from the beating. Yes suh, that's why I had to leave.

I walked from way over there to come to the church where I used to belong to. We was living above the church and then after he jumped me and everything, Grandpa and Grandma was living right there at the church, and I walked from there to Grandma's and Grandpa's. So I stayed down there a long time. Then Mama wanted me to come home and she come down there to get me, but I didn't want to go back. She knew what had happened. Yeah, Mama knew what had happened. I had told her.

He was plowing up in the field or something and Mama was hoeing some cotton I think it was and I was helpin'. So I said, "Mama." She said, "What." I said, "I got something to tell you." She said, "What is it?" I said, "If I tell you you'll whip me." She said, "If you don't tell me I'm gonna whip you." Just like that. So I went on and told her. I told her about how he did and what he said to me, you know.

Well, Mama throwed the hoe down and went across the field to where he was and she got onto him about it. Then he told

Georgianna Novella Hunt.
Photo by the author.

the mules "Whoa," and he stopped them. There was a big oak tree in the yard and he reached up there and got him several limbs and plaited them together and lit on me. Gave me a whippin'. Then he went in the house and picked up some of my clothes and throwed them out the window. And that's when I walked down to my grandmother's. I left because he beat me and told me to go. It was raining and I was hurtin' from the beatin'. Yes suh, that's why I had to leave. I went and stayed with my grandpa and grandma and Mama come down there trying to get me to come back. I was cryin' and didn't want to go back and that's when she picked up a piece of firewood and hit me in the head with it. So I run down there and waded through that branch and come up through the briar patch on up to Tin Cup where my aunt and uncle was. I didn't know if I could stay there or not but I knew they was my aunt and uncle. I ran up the back and I think the outhouse was sittin' there in the back. So I hid what little clothes I had in that toilet. But Uncle John saw me. So he said, "What was that you put out there in the toilet?" I wouldn't tell him so he went out there and got it and brought them to the house. So then I commenced to tellin' 'em what had happened. After I told them, they said, "Well you can stay here, you ain't goin' back." So they let me stay there.

Then my daddy from Philadelphia, he was married then, he come down and I had a big knot on my head and he wanted to know why. So I told him. He says, "I ain't got enough money to carry you back now. I'm goin' back now, but I'll send you a ticket." And he told Aunt Bertha and Uncle John to tag me and put me on the train. So they did and I went to Philadelphia. He was my real father, that's what Mama said, that's all I knowed. I was too small to ever knowed him before. But before I left, I lived there with my aunt and uncle for a while. Then after so long a time, Mama came over there after me, and I run from her all that day. She got the police after me to make me go home. I told the police what had happened and I didn't want to go home. So this policeman turned around and said, "Well if that's the case I ain't gonna make you go home," and he walked out. So Aunt Bertha and Uncle John took me to the station and tagged me and put me on the train. I wasn't old enough to ride the train by myself, so they had to put a tag on me and then my daddy met me at the station up there.

That was about 1919. I stayed up there with Daddy and his wife a little while, but Mama was still wanting me to come back home. She was still living over there in the country. Said she was sick and she wanted me to come home and take care of her. So I didn't stay that long in Philadelphia that time that Daddy sent for me. But you see, I went back to Philadelphia myself. I came home that time but I didn't stay with my mother. I think I went to stay with Aunt Bertha and Uncle John. I stayed here a good bit and then I went back to Philadelphia. I ain't been too long back from Philadelphia. I'd say about ten years, something like that. Well see, I came back from Philadelphia this time to take care of Mama. I took care of both of them, her and my stepfather, they was both sick. I loved my mother, I really did. My mother and I looked just alike, that's what they say. But when I left I didn't worry about it too much after what he did to me. Mama wrote a letter up to Philadelphia and said she was sick so my daddy didn't make me go back, but he said since she was sick he would let me come back. I was just a kid, and I didn't have a mind like could decide what to do.

So I came back, got married, and went to work in the tobacco factory. I don't know how old I was when I went in there but I was real young. Just a youngun. Yeah, R.J. Reynolds Tobacco Factory in Winston-Salem. When I first started I think I was working on the stemming machine. Stemming tobacco, you know, you untie the tobacco and lay it down here and then you cut the stems off. You run it through the machine and the stem would come off and come through a belt. Yeah, I done that. It wasn't such hard work for me, not back then, but it was dirty. You know, the dust. With the machines running it was dusty. There was mens and girls working with me, all black. While I was working there, I had one child and it lived five days and died.

But all that's behind me now. Since I come back I got this

house from May Davis. She let me have this house for two thousand dollars. So I'm gonna stay right here and live for Jesus. I'm gonna live for Him, now that's the truth. I'm gonna keep my hand right in His'n. That's the truth. Yes indeed. All that other stuff is done away with. I don't worry about it no more. I done got too young for it. Yes suh, got too young for it. I've found Jesus, yes suhree.

MARRIAGE, MOTHERHOOD, AND WORK

In the early twentieth century, the social expectations of the southern poor or working-class white woman included marriage, which meant leaving home at a tender age; motherhood, which meant birthing as many children as her body could produce; and work, which meant matching her husband's labor and supplementing his income whether in the fields or in the mills. To remain unmarried lowered the woman's status within her community and placed a burden on her family. Girls were often pushed into marriage and out of the home to make room for the younger children. With no knowledge of birth control or, for that matter, any idea of how the female reproductive system worked, women had no control over the number of children they bore. As a result families as large as twelve to twenty children were not unusual. If a husband proved unable or unwilling to work for whatever reason, the results were devastating for his wife and family. It meant that the wife was responsible for farming the land, raising the children, *and* maintaining the home. Even when the man worked, the labor of his wife was essential in the fields to produce enough crops for the family to stay alive. Often the woman was the main one in the fields. Coming from this kind of desperate lifestyle, it is no wonder that southern women responded in such large numbers to the opportunity for cash labor in the mill villages. For many white southern women, mill work provided a degree of economic independence. For the first time, a woman had a way out of a mentally or physically abusive marriage, because the mill provided a way for her to be financially independent of her husband.

This did not mean that the single mill woman lived a more comfortable life than before, except perhaps for the peace of mind she found in coming home from work and being boss in her own home. The early twentieth-century mill woman still worked a sixteen-hour day in the mill and maintained her home, at least until her oldest children were of age to enter the mill. Then she left the mill and the family lived on the wages of the children while the mother worked in the home. This pattern, in which the mill woman received some reprieve from overwork, changed when child labor laws prohibited children from working in the mills.

The second generation of mill women, who had begun work as young children and as a result had received little if any education, were then forced to carry on as the sole support of their families until their children were grown. Even with a husband and the eight-hour day, mill work pressed the southern woman beyond what could be reasonably expected of anyone. Just as she was expected to work when she married, she was also expected, in an overwhelming number of homes, to be responsible for the rearing of the children and the housework.

Poor diets and heavy work caused a high rate of illness among mill women and, coupled with the responsibilities for taking care of others who were sick, caused women to lose substantially more working time than did men. Indeed, women died on the job at a significantly higher rate.

When asked why so many mill women remained in the same jobs rather than demanding to be part of management, retired mill woman Blan Kilpatrick of Kannapolis said, "We felt lucky to have any kind of job at all in the mill. Back then if we had demanded to be supervisors or anything like that, we would have been laughed out of there." In other words, entry into the mill itself marked what was thought to be a radical enough progression for southern white women. Except for family size, this way of life continues today for the southern mill woman. Working at

some of the same jobs as my grandmother and my greatgrand-
mother, mill women are still stuck in the most menial positions
at the mill, and they are still earning among the lowest wages in
this country.

ALIENE WALSER

Thomasville, North Carolina

I didn't have no family before I was married. My mother died when I was five, my father died when I was six, and I was switched here and yonder and everywhere. My mother's sister was mainly responsible for raising me. There were thirteen children in her family—three girls and ten boys. She kept me from the time I was five years old until I was ten. Then she said she couldn't keep me no more. Well, they brought me over here to the Baptist orphanage and tried to put me in that orphanage home. But they said my mother and father had died of tuberculosis, so they wouldn't take me. We had to have x-rays every six months, me and my two brothers. Honey, I can't tell you what a bad experience that was, living with my aunt. I would wake up crying for my mother and daddy at night and she'd turn the cover back and whip me. She'd whip me and shut me in the closet. Now I'm scared of getting into somewhere I can't get out of. That's the way I was treated. Then my aunt said she didn't want me no more, that they couldn't keep me no longer. So I went to stay with my grandmother and I stayed there about a year before she said that she couldn't keep me.

My brother was five years older than me and he didn't have nowhere to go. He used to sleep on porches. He'd come to my aunt's house where I was staying and sit down to eat dinner and she'd run him away from the table. I never will forget that. He would get up crying and leave. Finally, when my brother got married, I came to live with them in Thomasville. His wife and him separated when I was fourteen years old, so I quit school and went to housekeeping for this family who had four children. Two dollars a week for cooking and scrubbing. That's when I met my husband Anderson. When me and him was dating, before we was married, we had to take the children with us, so we've been with children before we were married and ever since.

Then one day I decided to go back home. So they got me back down there below Denton, and I stayed one night with my uncle—I knew I couldn't live there—and then I hired my uncle to bring me back, and me and Anderson went to Virginia to get married. Got one of my friends to go with me. He was seventeen and I was fourteen, but Anderson told them in Virginia that he was twenty and that I was eighteen. I had on my first pair of high-heel shoes. I never will forget trying to walk up them courthouse steps. And honey, I could stand under your arm, I didn't weigh but seventy-four pounds. Well, the magistrate looked at us and he said, "You younguns go home." So we come back home. See, I didn't have no one to sign for me. So his mother and one of his aunts and us went to the courthouse in Lexington and got our license. They signed for us and we came back to Thomasville. Preacher James out here on Fisher Ferry Street married us. That night, I'd say we got married about one-thirty in the afternoon, at four o'clock he went in to work at the mill. The girl who lived across the street came over there and she liked to pick and joke, and oh, she had me scared to death that she was going to crawl under my bed and going to do this and going to do that. She embarrassed me to death.

Then we lived with his parents in a mill house over there on Concord Street right behind the mill. It had six rooms. We had two rooms, a kitchen and a bedroom. His parents lived in the other rooms. That was all right, Anderson's mother was like a mother to me. We lived there until my first baby was born. When I was pregnant for the first time, I was sitting there sewing with my mother-in-law one night and I said, "I wouldn't mind having this baby if I didn't have to have my stomach cut open." She looked at me and said, "Honey, you mean that you don't know

Aliene Walser about the time of her marriage.
Photo courtesy of Aliene Walser.

no better than that and fixin' to have a baby?" I said, "What do you mean?" And when she told me I said, "Ain't no way I'm going to go through that." That like to have scared me to death. See, I didn't understand anything about my body. If I had, I wouldn't have had so many children.

The first time I ever started my period I was going to the spring to get a bucket of water. I was living with my brother and his wife then. All at once I looked and blood was going down my leg and it scared me to death. I didn't know what to do. I ran in the house and told my brother's wife and she told me what to do. She said for me to go in there and get something to put on. I was ashamed to tell my grandfather. And that was all that was ever said to me about it. That's all I ever knowed. She told me that it would happen again. I said, "What for?" She never did explain nothing like that to me. Didn't nobody.

I had my first two babies at home. His mother was there and she fixed my bed and told me to get in it. She helped me put on my gown and she would always have pads just about this wide, about four feet across, and she would put a lot of cotton padding in it to use under me. That way they could be thrown away afterwards. Then she called the doctor. And I laid there in pain until he got there. They didn't give you anything for the pain, you know. I remember that doctor sitting there and me hurting so bad. He was sitting there beside my bed and he went off to sleep! So I kicked him. Then after my first baby was born I told him I never was having another one, this was my last. And then, when my second one came along, he looked at me and said, "I thought you weren't going to have another one."

I was fifteen when I had my first baby and thirty-two when I had my eighth. I raised seven of them. No, I didn't know how *not* to have babies. If I had known, I don't think I would have had eight. No, I never heard tell of birth control pills. Lordy mercy, honey, them things come out since I quit having kids. I wish I had had them back then. Maybe I wouldn't have been so tired.

I went to work in the cotton mill in 1940. I remember I was scared to death. I knowed I was doing everything wrong. I was scared the boss man would say something to me. I was actually scared to death! I didn't do anything wrong but I thought I was doing everything wrong. I was running a winder and it was called a spool winder. It had wooden tubes on it that were long and the thread went around it. When you first start them off that metal makes an awful racket. Well, I didn't know that. First time I had ever run them. Well, when I started that thing up and it started making this horrible noise, I run out of the alley and started crying like a baby. The boss man come up and said, "What's the matter?" And I said, "I've torn that thing up." Finally some women that worked around me got me calmed down and told me that it always does that. I got used to that noise finally, but I never did like to run that machine.

I stayed in the mill until World War II. Then my husband went into the service and my brother moved in with me because the children were small and I was pregnant again. I had my baby on the ninth and my husband left to go into the service that day. After he took his training, they sent him overseas. He didn't even get to come home to see the youngest until she was two years old. I waited until my baby was about four months old and then my brother's wife took care of the children so I went to work at the Erlanger Mill in Lexington. My sister-in-law taught me to wind over there. Then my husband came home and we moved down close to Charlotte. I went to work in a mill down there in the winding room. We stayed down there six years and then we came back to Thomasville. I went back to work in the Amazon Cotton Mill as a winder and I worked I don't know how many years winding. Then I was switched from that to running twisters. I don't know if you know what twisters are, but it twists yarn together, nylon and wool. I worked on that job for about four years. Then they put me to keeping the time sheets and stamping yarn and keeping what pounds the people would get off. You know, they got paid by the pound. I'd been there so long, I knew it all by heart.

There were better jobs, yeah. Some of them were happy doing the same old job day in and day out but I wasn't. I wanted more money. There were men all around me doing jobs that were easier than what I was doing and they were making more money. That bothered me. My husband was a boss man out there for a good long while, but I don't care if he was, when Christmas-time came around, the men got a big bonus and we women might get a little one. I just didn't think that was fair. We had to work as hard as the men. Harder! They were sitting on their rears writing down numbers. They said it was brain work. And I said, "What brain?" Yeah, I know I was working hard. Some of them were afraid to say anything though. See, they were scared they would lose their jobs, I reckon. And they probably would have. Mill people take a lot. But you'll find one or two that's not like that. They put me working with this man one time and he'd come in of a morning and maybe he'd be a little grouchy. I'd say, "Now listen here, I feel bad too, so get your butt off your shoulders." That's what I'd tell him and he'd start laughing at me.

Before I was married, I remember hearing that mill people wasn't nothing but slum people, that there wasn't nothing to them. I've heard it said that mill people are a lower class of people. A lot of them that worked at the furniture factory thought that they was better than mill workers. I got about seven or eight uncles that worked there and I know. They thought they was better than mill people and still do. I didn't know whether that was true or not until I went to work in the mill and learned the truth. There's a lot of good people working in there. I've got friends that work in the mill and they have been good to me. Those that think we're a lower class of people ought to go in the mill and find out for themselves, if they got sense enough to do the work. People were moving in and out all the time on mill hill. Different types that drank, fuss and fight, and goings on. But now there was some real good people on the mill hill. You could have real good neighbors. They would do anything in the world for you, they could.

We wanted to own our own home, but we had seven children to put through high school. I cooked three meals a day, forty biscuits for each meal. I got to where I knew how to make that

Aliene Walser, 1984.
Photo by the author.

bread so that it would be forty biscuits every time. And they would eat it up. We ate a lot of beans and potatoes and had meat about three times a week. On Sundays always. I tried to raise my girls differently than how I had been raised. I tried to tell them when they first started wanting to date that I didn't want them to start dating early, which they didn't. They said, "But Mama, you did." And I'd say, "Yes, but I don't want you to do what I done." I said, "I got married when I was just a child. You need to get a little more out of life than just getting married, having children, and working in that mill." I explained to my girls about going with boys and things like that, and having babies and things like that. We just talked about it like there wasn't nothing to it. There was some of my boys that I even talked to. My youngest one I did, about going with girls. I said, "You might think that if something happened to a girl you was going with, it wouldn't be on you," but I said it would. "You've got to be careful with girls. Anything like that you need to have marriage first before you think about it, because," I said, "anything could happen and you might have to get married. And them kind of marriages sometimes just don't work out." Yeah, I tried to bring them up in the church which I think I have, most of them. My youngest son used to have a temper like nobody's business, but now he goes to Liberty Baptist. He got saved and now he's changed.

I didn't want my girls to have to work in the mill. I know people out there who have been hurt real bad on the job. I was working on the first shift and this woman was working on the second. She had long beautiful blonde hair and she bent over some way and her hair got caught in the machine. When it did, it just pulled her scalp off. They said blood was just pouring down her. Her boss man like to have passed out. They took her on to the hospital and sent somebody to go over there and get her scalp out of that thing and see if they could, you know, but nothing they could do. She stayed in the hospital for a long time. That happened about seven or eight years ago. Last thing I knew she was still going to the doctor's because she started having severe headaches. The insurance company fought it because they didn't want to pay off. So they took her to court. She didn't like for anyone to see her without her wig but they made her pull it off in court and they said she was crying. It was so pitiful.

I was working on second or third shift until the last job I had was on the first shift. My husband worked on one shift and I worked on the other. At the mill we had an understanding, he'd leave in time to get home so that I could get there in time to start work. Well, when I worked on the second shift, I'd sleep, say, about five hours a night. I have worked on third when I wouldn't get but three hours sleep. I worked on third one time and I wouldn't get no sleep at all because I would come in from work of a morning and I'd have to cook my breakfast and get the kids off to school. My husband was working on second. Then I'd do my wash or whatever I had to do and lay down maybe about ten thirty or eleven o'clock. Then I'd have to get up at two for him to get ready to go to work. I got my nerves so bad that time that my boss man told me I was going to have to go on another shift. I had gotten down to seventy-some pounds.

Then I worked on that shift until I was seven months pregnant with my last child. My boss man came and told me I was going to have to quit because they didn't want nobody in there after they were six months pregnant. They were scared something would happen and it would be on their hands. So I got a leave of absence for six months, but I didn't go back for six years. I just couldn't go back.

CELESTE KING

Kannapolis, North Carolina

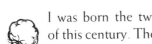 I was born the twenty-ninth day, and the twelfth year of this century. The place was called Shankletown, a little town opposite Concord. That's where I was born. I had five sisters and one brother. We were sharecroppers. See, back seventy years ago, sharecroppers moved a lot, you know, different places. When I was old enough to remember, we was living up towards Mooresville. Yeah, my daddy used to move every year just about. Well, I don't know exactly how it was then, but maybe one boss, farm owner, you know, would give you more for farming, you know, like you'd work for a third. When I was born my daddy owned horses. He was a sharecropper but back then if you'd have your own stock and things to work with, you'd make more money working the other man's ground. And that's the reason we moved so much, trying to make more money.

When I was ten years old, my mother and father was divorced. I went to live with my great uncle and aunt, and they raised me up until I was able to take care of myself, you know, go out on my own, until I was seventeen. The other kids went to Salisbury with my mother. Well, before my mother married my daddy, she lived with these people, the Weatherspoons, and she had promised them that when she had her first child, her and my daddy, that if ever anything came up, any disagreement between them and they didn't live together, that they could have me, that I could go and live with them. She promised them that. So whenever it happened, well, then, course they came and got me and

I went to live with them. I liked living with them, oh yes, they were just like my real mother and daddy. They really was sweet to me, treated me just like they did they children. I believe they raised eight out of fourteen. And I was treated just like one of them.

After finishing school in Mooresville, I went to high school at Scotia Seminary for two years. After that I went on to Statesville to live and work in a private home. That's what I did. If you had a parent that was able to pay for you to go, you could go to high school and college, 'cause right along then, I'd say about 1928, 1929, Kannapolis didn't have a black high school. They went to about the ninth grade. Mooresville was the same way for black people. They didn't have the same opportunity as white people. They didn't have that opportunity.

Going back to my real daddy, he always would help me when I went to live with the Weatherspoons. And he would do what he could for me. So he paid for my tuition fees for me to go down there to Scotia. I reckon the Weatherspoons would have done it but having a bunch of children of they own, you know, and several of them younger than I was, they had to take care of them. You didn't make but so much money on the farm at that time as a sharecropper. I believe it cost about three hundred dollars a school year to go to Scotia. If you were a fast learner, you always had encouragement to do something like that, and I was always a fast learner. When I was in the third grade, the teacher told me I read on an eighth-grade level. So having things like that, you didn't have money, but they was always somebody behind you encouraging you or encouraging your parents. Now the children where I was raised up with, they was slow learnin', so everybody in the neighborhood and in the church, you know, they was behind me one hundred percent for them to send me to Scotia if they could. I never read that much. I guess I was just born gifted. That's what I would say. Before I was ever old enough to go to school, I could count to a hundred. I knew the multiplication tables through about I'd say five. I knew the Roman tables to one hundred. My daddy taught me how to tell time one afternoon in about thirty minutes. The way he did it, he said,

"When the long hand is on the twelve and the short hand is on the twelve, that's twelve o'clock. And when the long hand gets on one, that's five minutes after." And he went on down the line until he got on down to six and he said, "That's twelve thirty." Then when he started at seven, he said that's 'til one, on up 'til he got to one o'clock. He did that two or three times and I could do it behind him. All I could say is that I was just gifted to it, because you only had to show me about once or twice and I could do it.

But I didn't get to go on through school. I had bad luck. You know how it is when little boys get in the way of books. That's two things that don't go together. That's boys and books. You know, little sweethearts. So I had a sweetheart while I was at Scotia. Then I had this child. That would be my oldest child. He's never married 'til yet. I was very near eighteen when I had him. I come out of school to have my child, and see I didn't get to go back and finish. See, I could have finished and been able to teach around here, see, in these little country schools. But then after that I didn't get to go back and I had to go to work to support myself and my child. I felt bad about it, that's how I felt, but there was nothing I could do about it. When I found out that I was pregnant I knew my life was going to change. Yes, I certainly did. And I reckon my foster parents didn't have the patience. Maybe if I had been with my real mother and father, but they didn't have a home to take me. Daddy was living with white people what he worked for on the lot up here in the country. Wasn't nothing he could do but help support me wherever I got to live, so I had to leave the Weatherspoons then and get out on my own. And that's what I did. I been on my own ever since.

I went to work in Statesville, working in private homes. There wasn't too much else for black people to do at the time. I worked for a doctor for two or three years. Then I worked in a private home for some white people that owned a furniture factory, and I stayed there thirteen years. Then I decided I wanted to come home. Back in Mooresville and Kannapolis. I stayed in Mooresville until 1951, and I been in this vicinity ever since. I lived on the place when I worked in private homes. They had private places, servant's quarters. First I worked for this doctor, and then these other people what were wealthy. Still this was a comedown from my dreams. I had always wanted to be a schoolteacher and, yeah, this kind of knocked a hole in it. I remember that year I quit school quite well, because that was the time during the Depression and it was very tough. But I made it. I wasn't depressed. I've always been a churchgoer. I've always gone to church ever since I could remember. I'd read my Bible and I've always depended on that, and believed in the Bible. So that got me through it. It certainly did.

My child, his grandfather and his grandmother on his father's side, they took him. Lord, I couldn't have raised him, you didn't get but about two or three dollars a week. I worked for this doctor back in the 1930s when the bank went rupted and I got two dollars a week. They'd write me a two-dollar check. I had to work every other Sunday. They had a little boy and I had to keep him on Sunday. They didn't go to church but they would go fishin' or something like that. Then when I went to these other people who owned the furniture factory in '35, they gave me four dollars a week. And that was about what you got. I'd say five dollars a week was the best you could get at that time working in a private home. And then I quit working for them in '45, that was the year Roosevelt passed. I was married and the people I was working for had houses because he owned this factory. I was pregnant so we stayed on there in one of his houses. I lost that baby. When I quit I was making twenty-five dollars a week, not counting my tips. He owned this factory and men from up the road would come down and would be going on south or something, and he'd call me at the last minute and tell me to put down another plate, you know, he was having so-and-so for dinner, and then they'd leave me good tips. But I quit when I got married.

I met my first boyfriend when we was kids. We used to pick peas together when we was six or seven years old. They'd make us sacks out of flour sacks, you know, sew little straps on the shoulder and we'd put the peas in the sack crossways so they'd fill up quick and we'd run to the pile where we'd throw them on and empty our sacks, and we'd have us a good time. Yeah, we grew up together. We could holler at each other's home down in the country. That's how close we lived together. Yeah, we played on them peas. I know we shelled them peas. They was on a big old sheet, they'd sew two sacks together and sew big sheets to pile the peas on, and we'd play on 'em. They'd make us stop and come on back to work and we wasn't doing nothing but playing.

Yeah, childhood sweethearts. But I never did want to get married, and I never did want no children. I would say it was on account of a broken home. See, my home was a broken home. My mama and daddy used to fuss and you know how that will grow up in a child. It'll make you not want to go through the same thing. You might think it might be the same thing. I would have no way knowing that mine wasn't going to be just like theirs. There wasn't too much said about getting married back then. You didn't have too much to get married with. Now that's the truth. To this day, I love being independent and love staying by myself. I don't know, it just seems like I'm contented or something or another. I don't know, I just like to be by myself. My grandson who lives with me went to Alabama to his aunt's last month and stayed three weeks, and I was the happiest thing. I didn't have to pick up, I didn't have to cook for him, I didn't have to wash his clothes. A lot of them says, "Celeste, why don't you get married again." I don't want to get married no more. No-o-o, I don't want to get married no more.

I didn't get married until April of '47. Now I didn't like soldiers all that much, but I felt sorry for them or something or another and I used to exchange letters with them, you know, in the different camps they was in and when they was overseas. I would get their addresses out of the *Afro*, a Negro newspaper, and I would exchange letters with them and everything. My husband was from Mooresville, Lake Norman way, on the other side of Mooresville. That's where he was raised. But we were on a ferry boat when I met him. And we started writing. Then, seemed like he signed up for three or four more years and they sent him back

Celeste King, 1984.
Photo by the author.

overseas. So while he was over there and we was writing letters back and forth, he wrote and asked me to marry him. And I answered the letter and said yeah. Oh Lord. I was about thirty-three. Well, I reckon I felt sorry for him.

But I decided I'd get married. Try it, you know, and it was all right. We been married about thirty-five years and I'd say out of that, I lived with him for about eight years. To tell you the truth, he wouldn't work. Before he went into service, he used to work seven days a week. I think the army did something to him, now that's the truth. When he came out of the army, he didn't care whether he worked or not. No responsibility. And a married man! Somebody got to have some responsibility, 'cause I couldn't work and have the babies too. So we didn't have no kind of words, no kind of fallin' out or nothing. I told him, I said, "I can't carry this load by myself." I said, "You go your way and I'll go mine if you don't want no responsibility." So that's what we did. We still friends. I mean, he would come and see me. Not as no dating friend or nothing like that, but we never did have no trouble about him with another woman or me with another man. We act more like brother and sister. Just friends. I raised five children out of six, 'cause I lost the first one. Premature birth. That was in the fifties and I was still doing housework. Day work or pay by the week. I didn't live in then. I would try to get a job where there was transportation to and from home.

I had help with raising my children. I had help now. I had a large family. My daughter was raised in Statesville and I raised the rest of 'em by myself. 'Cause when I came here to live in '51, I got a job as head cook at a boarding house. It was run by a widowed lady, Mrs. Thunderbird, and she had two children that she was raising up. She helped me a lot. She'd give me food to bring home for my sons and daughters. When I started buying this little house and I had the mortgage payments, if I didn't have the payment together, she'd go ahead and pay it and take it out of my salary. She helped me a lot and I worked for her nineteen years and missed two days—one day I went to a funeral and one day I had a cold. Out of nineteen years I was out two days.

Whenever you try to do right or do the best you can, somebody will help you. I always had that figured. So I got 'em up and sent one of my sons to Livingston Seminary, and Linda Jo, my baby, she got a four-year scholarship to A&T in Greensboro, academically.

I've always had a good job. Always had a good job. I love to work and I'd be working right now if I didn't have arthritis in this right knee. That's all that's keeping me here now. I left the boarding house because Mrs. Thunderbird said her and myself was getting too old to cook and for her to transact business. We fed over a hundred people a day, mostly mill workers. I did two-thirds of the cooking myself. I made pies and over 250 biscuits a day. I mean made 'em up in a big bowl, rolled 'em out, and cut 'em out. Pies, I'd make twenty-five or more. Fry great big boxes of steak and twenty-five to thirty chickens a day. But Mrs. Thunderbird said she was just going to quit because the people didn't want her to keep going up with the prices, see, and everything was getting high. So she said she was going to give it up. So when she quit feeding, she had somebody to do like the beds and work like that. I didn't have to go no further than the kitchen and the dining room. What I did was do the cooking, prepared the meals, and I did the collecting. The people what come to eat, they paid me. I had a money box on the table. So after she quit feedin' she didn't need me. So first I went down here in front of the hospital and went to a bakery, and worked in a bakery for about a year.

Yeah, before the mills opened up for black women, all they had was washing and ironing and cooking for white people. That's about all I can think, nothing else. Not to my knowledge, not that was worth anything.

Now, I've always thought that I should have had a better break in life than what I had. But I always felt like it was my fault. I felt like I should have kept my head straight, see what I'm talking about, but I got out of line. I felt like the mistreatment like I got, it was my fault. The bad breaks that I got in life, I don't hold nobody responsible but myself. 'Cause I feel like my daddy would have gone on and tried to help me get through school if I hadn't gotten pregnant. Then I could have got a good-paying job. So I carried some guilt around with me. Yeah, sure did, but I still feel like it was all on me. I don't have no hard feelings towards nobody. Then sometimes I think, well, maybe it was not meant to be. If it had, seem like it would have worked out.

BILLIE PARKS DOUGLAS

Kannapolis, North Carolina

I was born June 4, 1928, in Cabarrus County. My mother was Anne L. Parks. She married Mason Parks and there was seven of us. My mother was a teacher long time ago when it was unusual for a black woman to be a teacher. My mother was a smart woman. She would give these phenomenal addresses, speeches like, to me nobody could give. I didn't have the privilege of hearing her much, but when I did, she would go in all the churches, white and black, where she would deliver these messages, and they would be fantastic. She wasn't considered a preacher. She spoke, maybe like I do. Mostly my ministry is to women. Things like Women's Day and Mother's Day. Those are usually the kind of occasions that I speak on. We have a missionary program to encourage women, and usually my message is to the women. I hope, like for black women in the South, the message I give is an encouraging message. That we don't have to roll over and lay down and die.

I always wanted to be a missionary but in my family they was seven of us when I was coming up. The one to finish school would be the oldest. That one became the teacher. I happened to not be the oldest. Well, they didn't have the money for all of us and education wasn't available then like it is now. But I always wanted to go to Africa.

I had a good childhood and I had a good mother and father. And we younguns didn't know that we was poor until they told us on television. We really didn't. My mother and daddy never made us feel like we was poor.

We slept three to the bed and until today I can't sleep on my back because they made me sleep in the middle. I was the littlest, you know, and I didn't want to sleep with my face in theirs so I had to lay on my back with my face looking right up into the sky. But we had a good time. Now we didn't have a lot of things, but we jumped rope and we always had a bicycle together, and we had a good family relationship.

Then they started talking about the poverty-stricken area. You know all this stuff came out, when? Yeah. In the sixties. Well this was the area that was designated as the poverty-stricken area. We were shocked. We just laughed because we didn't know.

People won't believe this, but I never heard my mother and father quarrel. Now, some of the older ones mighta, I know they must have quarreled, but evidently they'd get in a room and do whatever they had to do, because we never heard them. I was the baby until I was nine years old and I was pretty spoiled because, you know, what happens when you got a whole lot of big brothers and sisters. Plus I was the teacher's child. Then black teachers was rare.

I went to school when I was younger than the rest of the people, and at school is where I met my husband. I remember he was a couple of years older than I was and I was at the board and I was to add fifteen and fifteen and I could not learn to carry that one. I stood at that board and I cried and, he don't re-member this, but the teacher told him to go up and show me how to carry that one. I was about six and he was about eight. Now it was years and years later that I came to know him better. I was eighteen when we got married. I had one child before I was married and we had nine children. I had my first child when I was sixteen and my tenth when I was twenty-nine. Some of them are the same age for a few months, so I had some of them less than a year apart. I worked at that time at the Wincoff school, went in washing pots and then I went to cookin'. I worked there for thirteen years and I'd quit around July to have my babies and then would go back in September. I was fortunate, I didn't have to have nobody to watch my children, because I had this sister-in-law who would always babysit for me. Then, when the kids'd go to school I'd go to work at eight and get home at two-thirty.

Now I wanted to be a missionary and go to Africa. Oh, I thought I could do great things, but it didn't work out that way. When I had my first child, I dropped out of school to have her, and then I went back the next year. I dropped out at the end of the year and what they did they gave me a make-up test and I made the work up and went on back the next year. I was going to Landis School at the time. So when I went back I went to the Kannapolis school. That was the year that they added the twelfth grade. So you could finish in the eleventh or you could go on to the twelfth grade. That year you had a choice. I graduated in the eleventh at the top of my class. But that wasn't saying nothing because I think the smart ones went on to the twelfth.

When we moved down here to Fishertown, all the black kids walked down here three miles to Kannapolis to go to school. White kids came right by on the bus, you know, riding to school. When we came over here, my mama said you won't walk a step, not a day. You will not walk a step to school. And my father would say, "Annie, well now, you know you can't buck society." And my mother said, "They will not walk a step." She started making the rounds to the different schools, talking to different people. Like I said, she was a good talker. She went to Rowan County. We lived in Cabarrus County, you know, but she went to Rowan County and the professor at that time was Professor Ellis and he was a smart man, and two weeks after we moved over here the bus started coming by to pick us up from Rowan County and we went to Rowan County School.

My first job after finishing school was probably baby-sitting. But I had worked before that. We would go to work and stay on the lot, back when I was about fourteen years old. I didn't do a whole lot of work. Mama didn't make us work. I'd go and baby-sit in mill workers' houses, those that were on the second and third shift. And I think we made something like three dollars a week. That was about the 1940s, the early forties. See that was all that you knew, so it was okay, I mean, that was what you did.

We didn't have any other choices. We didn't harbor any ill feelings because we didn't know nothing else, and we'd fall in love with those kids and they would love you. You'd raise those children, you'd take care of those children, you'd play with those children, and sometimes they'd cry to come home with you. The mother would be just a little bit jealous of your relationship with that child. But then when my children were born, I didn't exactly resent it, like I say, but I would try to do for my child because it seemed like I would be away from mine all day taking care of somebody else's and usually when you got home you'd have all this sympathy for your own child.

These white women taught me how to clean house because I had older sisters who did all the work at home and so I didn't learn to do it. So they literally taught me how to clean house when I was fifteen and sixteen years old. How to rake the crumbs off the table without getting the crumbs all over the floor. But I didn't resent my job. Back then you was just happy you had a job. You didn't know anything else. This is just what everybody did.

Now I didn't go to work in the mill for some time. Because they didn't 'low no black women in there. I remember we used to walk by the mill and we'd think, you know, if I was in there we could get well. If I could bring a check like that home we could all get well. Yes, we resented it. You know, they would probably pay us for a week with what they made in a day, and sometimes less, and of course we resented it. But that was what we was used to and we did what we had to do. Now I never envied mill people, but I've heard my daughter Mavis say that she wished she could dress like they dress and do things like go to the beach. See, we was struggling by at home, we had to. See, we didn't have the opportunity to live in those houses at that time. Way years later they opened the mill houses up to black people and then they'd be down in a holler or way back in something. My mama and daddy built their own house. See, we'd have carpenters, and everybody did what they had to do for themselves. They'd pitch in together and buy the lumber and build each other's houses. We resented it when we found out that mill workers were living in those houses almost free and here we were struggling along. I mean they didn't go around telling people about it back then but when we found out, yeah, we resented it.

I didn't go to work in the mill until '62, about a year after they opened it up to black women. But I was making pretty good money before I went to work in the mill. I was making about thirty-five dollars or forty dollars a week where I was, plus I didn't have to leave my children. I was working for these people who had this daughter-in-law who was extravagant, and she worked in this pajama factory and I remember one time she gave me fourteen pairs of pajamas. I was always blessed like that. I worked with all these white women that—like Mavis, my daughter, said—she didn't know how they could have so many clothes. And they gave me good clothes. What I would do is wash those clothes, iron and pack them back, and at Easter time my children looked as pretty as anybody else. Plus I learned to sew, so my kids got along. They didn't have no three or four pairs of shoes—they probably didn't have but one pair of shoes. I liked that job because when those kids were out of school for three months I was out of work and could be with my children. Now I made better money in the mill but that job worked out good for me. After a while though, I just needed more money because the children were getting older.

I started out with a job that's about the same job I have now. Course you always had to go on third shift because of seniority. I've done just about everything in the card room. Hard. That's the best description of my job that I know. Hard. I run a machine where you got big cans of cotton on rollers about this high and you go behind the machine and you creel it in, you creel each one in about twice a night.* You got three machines on the back

---

*A creel is a bar that holds a bobbin
on a spinning machine. Used here to
describe a carding operation, creel
means to thread through.

and four on the front that you run. Now the front ones run so fast that it takes an extra back one to keep up with it. And the front ones creel about every hour and a half. Every job in the mill you got to creel and doff, but I'm not a creeler or a doffer. I'm a draw hand. That's the title of my job.

Okay, so I work with the drawing machines and they are great big machines and all it does is break down cotton, all the stuff in the cotton is sifted out. Okay. That's a card. Okay, the cotton goes from the card to the drawings which is still breaking down the cotton more and more, making it fine. What is done really is breaking the cotton down, making thread out of it. From the drawing machines it goes to another machine about as long as this house and there it's broken down even more until it's fine as a cord. Then it goes on down to the spinning room. Oh, it's dusty, the card room, I believe it's the dustiest place in the mill. It's very aggravating. Now they have masks that you can wear and they had goggles that you could wear to keep it from getting into your eyes. It's really dusty and the machines really get dusty and dirty.

When I went to work in the mill my oldest daughter, she was about twenty-two then, went in too. By that time my mother was sick, and the third shift was probably the best for me even though I couldn't have got another shift. Mama had hardening of the arteries and her memory was bad and that made her seem like she was off. Now Mama had been a really smart woman and all of a sudden she'd be forgetting everything. She lived down the street in a little house and we tried to make her leave, but you couldn't take her out of her home. We found that out because she went to stay with my sister, and Mama went way out in left field and she would be trying to go home all the time. So finally we took her back home. So I had that burden.

My husband did not help me. He worked as an aide at the veteran's hospital in Salisbury. He had a pretty good job but no, he didn't help here at home. You have to understand, black men now are changing. But then black men, they didn't help you with the children. Now I know a few who did, but for the most part they would just come home and do what they wanted to do and you had all that work to do. I did all the cooking because my husband didn't think children could cook. I don't even think he ever fixed his plate. I'd dip out the food and fix his plate and set it down before him. And then I didn't have an automatic washing machine. I was washing in a wringer-type washing machine and I'd be ironing in the living room and all across my big picture window I'd have these dresses and shirts. I'd cover the whole wall in the living room with my ironing. Because at that time they didn't have all these new materials that you don't iron. But my kids, they were different from children now. Children are children, they are mischievous and all that, but mine weren't hard to handle. I could pretty well depend on my children.

Then while I was working in the mill, I also sold World Books. That was the joy of my life 'cause I could get away. You know I liked to talk. I would sell books and that would supplement the income. I'd go to the black communities in Davidson, Concord, and I've been to Charlotte. I often wonder how I done it. I don't know but I did. I was tired every day. I literally thought I would never get rested. I went that way for years. Tired. One thing was that I could go to sleep back then where I can't now. When I hit the bed I could go right off to sleep. I've gone to sleep standing up. I have done it. I really have. I remember talking to my boss one time at the mill and I went to sleep in the middle of the conversation. I had myself trained. I said, "Let me get five minutes." Now if I could get five minutes, I could wake up and go for another hour. So I went in the bathroom and I slept for five minutes and I could wake up in five minutes. I had myself trained.

I have felt like leaving many a time. You know, me and my husband separated. Probably if it had not been for my children, I would have left. I would have been gone, but I didn't have that much time to feel like leaving, 'cause I was too busy. Before you know it, one day was gone and before you know it, it was another year and you was pregnant again. I mean, if you getting pregnant every year, how you gonna think about leaving?

I was much too busy with my family to think about leaving.

Billie Parks Douglas

We'd have prayer together and then, too, I'd take our family to
church picnics and outings. We'd play Monopoly, and Scrabble,
and we'd have cookouts, and I don't know where I'd have the
time but I found the time. Now, if a woman has two or three
children, they fall apart. They just so tired they can't go on, but
I done things with my children. I had things for my children just
like Mama had for us. And Christmas, okay, like I had ten children
and each one of them always got two things and I taught them
what to want. I would say, "Come here and tell me what you
want," and then I would teach them what to want. You know. I'd
get me a big catalogue and oh, we'd sit down and have the best
time looking at this catalogue and if I saw a doll that I could
afford I would fall in love with that doll. You know. And "Oh,
Mama, I want that doll, I want that doll." I did that and they were
happy. Couple of times I made a mistake and bought drums, but
I learned to teach them what to want. Then I would always get
them a surprise. Now if you think about having ten children and
everybody getting two things, I had a house full of toys.

We didn't have that much but I would cook and the house
would be filled with the aroma and I never had an artificial tree.
I always had a real tree from the ceiling to the floor. And people
would come and see that Christmas tree and we would decorate
that tree. My children sing real pretty, so we'd play the piano
and sing and we'd have a glorious time, you wouldn't believe it.
You really wouldn't believe it. And it didn't take that much money
to do it. But you have to know how to do it.

Yeah, we done things together. Now when my husband was
on second shift, like he worked from four to twelve and he'd get
home at one o'clock. Sometimes we'd be sitting up playing Monopoly, my neighbor and our children. No, we never neglected
our children. We'd do things that our children could do. We'd
go on these picnics. Today I hate picnics because then it took
so much work. We did it to keep them happy but I'd be so tired.
And there was no point in me thinking I was going on a picnic
and my husband was going to help me with the children, 'cause
he was going off fishing and going off with the boys. And, you

103

know, a baby on my lap and one on my knee and I'd be done fed up frying that chicken. So that now I don't like family reunions. I told my sister that but they fall apart if I don't go to them reunions. So I go. But I don't like them. And I didn't like them that well then but, you know, you do what you have to do in order to maintain your home.

Now you take eight girls and you have all those heads to do. Well, then we were into straightening our hair and we'd get out there in the back yard and we'd just have the best time. I'd be doing heads while we'd be playing. You know, I tried not to be complaining all the time about what I didn't like or what I didn't have. But once in a while I would get vexed. I got paid once a month. And every once in a while I'd just get mad and I'd go buy ribbons and boots and socks and all the things I wanted my children to have and just wouldn't pay nobody. Then I'd go on back to the mill and start paying bills again. I'd buy them all the things I thought they deserved because you'd see all these people coming in there with these food stamps and all this candy and stuff for their kids and they didn't own nothing. And here I was working hard and I couldn't get that for my kids. I'd just get fed up sometimes and I'd just go blow my money for those little things I wanted to buy. Then I'd get me a hat. I like hats so I'd go get me a hat. Then I'd feel good the next morning. I could go to work.

My daughter came home last Christmas and said, "Mama, this is why I like to come home, because you be doing things." You know, I fix up the house with little things. Everything would have a candle or some little old Christmas thing in it. Where everybody would buy cloth tablecloths, I would buy paper tablecloths, but we always had Christmas tablecloths. I always had the turkey and the ham, chitlins. I'd make five or six cakes at a time, at least. With the turkey you'd have dressing and green beans and then you'd have hot coffee and hot tea. We'd make Russian hot tea. And our friends would always come in. Now, when the children were small, they'd get up, see, and they'd be playing with their toys. Okay. The men would get their drinks. They'd go from house to house. It would be about one or two o'clock during the day. The ladies, they'd go from house to house and they'd drink coffee and they'd take something to eat. So, you know, we had a good time. We done a lot of laughing. We laughed a lot. And we could tell our jokes. For instance, the men and wives would get together and the men, they'd 'a had their drinks and we'd eat our cake and coffee because most of us didn't drink and the ones that did didn't drink at that time. Then we'd meet at somebody's house. Automatically, we'd all wind up at somebody's house and we'd have fun laughing and talking, playing Chinese Checkers or playing with the kids' toys. We always would say the men would buy the boys their toys so they could play with them. We had a good time.

It wasn't all that easy, though. It's sounding easier than it was. You had to fight for every ounce of it and like I said, in the meantime, Mama was sick. I think that was when things began to change between the whole family. I was preoccupied a lot. Of course the children took up a lot of my time and I had to neglect myself. I couldn't buy me things and the children things too, so what I did was neglect myself and do for the kids. That was just natural, I guess. And my husband, he was out there in the world and he seen all these women, you know, dressed good and looking good so his eyes began to rove and things. Meantime I never had any trouble with my kids, just one son I had a lot of trouble with. And that happened right along this time. I guess I was so preoccupied with myself and my problems that maybe I neglected to see what was going on with him at that time.

And you know all this took its toll. All these things was happening at the time when Mama was very sick and I was just really working hard. It just seemed like it was just personal to me. I had to take care of her, you know, and my husband, he would resent the time I would be spending with Mama 'cause she couldn't take care of herself. My sister, who helped me a lot, was old and pregnant at that time. And my brother had done all he could do. My sister just couldn't do for Mama at that time. Oh, she has told me how she wanted to just go and die with that last baby.

So things wasn't good. Then I was in a bad automobile wreck coming home from work. I had three kids then that was in college

Billie Parks Douglas, 1984.
Photo by the author.

at the same time, so you could imagine the struggle that was going on at that time. I was working in the mill then. The day my daughter was to go to Johnson C. Smith University was the day I came home from that automobile accident. So you know that was kind of a bad time. I had my leg broken in two places and a slipped disk which didn't show up 'til two months later. I tell you, I went to comb my mother's hair one day and I bent over and I couldn't straighten up. Meantime I was worried about my marital problems and I came out of the hospital with high blood pressure and it was the worry and the stress. First one thing and then the other. See, all that was going on around in the seventies.

How I made it through all that, well, I give God the credit. That's an old cliché but I give God the credit. Like I say, I was in and out of the hospital with high blood pressure and worry, and one day I was walking up to the house, coming in the back door worrying about Mama, really now, that was what was most important on my mind. Now my house was full and what I really wanted to do was bring her up here so I could really just take care of her and I couldn't do that. Her house wasn't fit to live in. The doors had caved in and it needed to be fixed up and you know how these old houses were, just thrown together. So I wanted to get her out of that and she didn't want to get out of it.

So, we would have family meetings when a crisis would come up. I would just gather my children together and we would talk. Okay. So I had this meeting. And I told my children, now Mama's got to be taken care of and I asked them if they would be willing to help if we was to get the house fixed up. Okay. My brother had children and my sister had children and another sister had children and I had all ten of these. So I had it fixed so that we would be with Mama one weekend out of seven. The children would help share the time with us. So that way Mama could be home where she could be happy.

So I went down to my brother's, and I didn't have no money, you know I didn't, and I asked him, I said, "Will you lend me your signature?" And he said, "What you got on your mind?" And I told him that I wanted to fix Mama's house. At that time Mama was staying with my sister and she would just go on out in left field and she'd be walking away to go back home, and, you know, just kept us in an uproar all the time. So I said to my brother, "You know we got to get Mama back home." So he said, "What's your plan?" I said a friend of my husband's said he would fix the house for nothing if you could get the material they needed. That was like at about twelve o'clock and at two o'clock he laid the money in my lap. When we fixed the house, the children went down there and enjoyed it so much that the grownups never did have to go. Course I was in and out constantly. I did the cooking for her. She had a big wood stove and I'd go down there and build a fire in the mornings. But it worked out good 'cause the kids, they would stay down there.

So I don't know how I got through that time, but somehow I did. I had a couple good friends. I don't think I could have got through it if it hadn't been for Verdie and Mildred. Sometimes when I would be depressed, I'd just pick up the phone and say, "Verdie, Mama was sick today," and she'd say, "I'll be up there in a little bit." And she'd come and just hold my hand. We'd be sitting in the living room until one o'clock at night. And all I'd have to say was, "Verdie, Mama was sick," and she'd say, "I'll be there in a little bit." And my husband's sister. You know, you'd think with the trouble that me and my husband was having at that time, and we was having some bad times, that she wouldn't have given me the support that she did. I mean she loved him, but she was support for me too. Mama used to tell me, "Billie, in this life if you got one good friend, one friend, you will have done good." Well, I think I've had four that I could sit there and pour my heart out to and trust them not to tell me what I wanted to hear but to tell me what's good for me. And who probably got tired of hearing it but would listen anyway. I think that's what got me through it. You know, they'd cry with me. That's how I got through it.

If I could relive my life again starting at sixteen, I would get an education and probably be that missionary. And, as much as I love these children of mine, I wouldn't have ten children. Because, first place, it's not fair to the children. I see that now more than when they were younger. When they were younger, I could spread myself around, but as they got older we had nothing to give them. We gave them love, but I was just thinking that I have friends who would help their kids get a house or help them furnish the house or something and I see my children struggling now and I feel like I cheated them. I would change that. Not that I place that much value on money but I think that money is necessary in this world. Another thing I think I would do is teach my children how to marry. I always felt like, now, that's their choice. Now I would make some suggestions. I know I can't cram this down their throats but I would make some suggestions. We have some sheltered children around here who have never really had to get out and face the world and do for themselves that much. And that was a mistake. I wouldn't do it that way again.

I didn't want to have ten children. No-o-o, God. I tried birth control, but what I used hurt me. And when I would try to do something, my husband would object. See we were about pleasing these men. We just thought that was what we was. Oh, would I change things. We thought that was what we was supposed to do. My attitude on that has changed. See, 'cause I look back over my life and I'm not bitter, but I resent the fact that I done everything that I could. I gave up everything and I done without everything, but in the end he left. I feel like I done for nothing. He didn't have the patience to see it through. Now we could be having a good life, but he didn't have the patience or the time.

CLARA THRIFT

Thomasville, North Carolina

My first job was at the T-ville Diner. It was an old railroad car that Dalton Myers had bought for fifty dollars and dragged to a small lot on West Main Street. He had sold the iron out from under it to buy the booths and equipment and added on a kitchen in the back. You went through a screen door that had a "Drink Cheerwine" sign on it, and behind the counter right up above the snuff and chewing tobacco was a sign that said "No Drinking." Davidson County was dry then and is today. We served fried chicken, pork chops, country-style steak. Then we'd have cream potatoes, french fries, black-eyed peas, cressie greens, or turnips. Stuff like that. We never wrote no orders down, just remembered them and hollered them out. I worked there from the time I was fourteen 'til I was eighteen. By that time I had a baby and Dalton would let me bring her with me when I didn't have a baby-sitter. She'd sit right there by that screen door next to the juke box in a highchair. I'd keep her supplied with creamed potatoes with stew beef gravy and she'd be just as happy sitting there smearing them potatoes all over herself and the juke box.

In 1950, when my baby was a year old, I went to work at the Carolina Underwear Company. My sister-in-law, Inez, was working there and she got me the job. So I went in, didn't know nothing about sewing, but I was going to learn because she was making some money and that's what I wanted to do. I wasn't living with Mama no more. I had got my own place. At the

Carolina Underwear, my job was called bar-tacking, and I worked as hard as I could to make production, which paid eight dollars a day. I thought that was big money back then. I started out at eighty-five cents an hour, but it wasn't long before the one dollar an hour came in. That was minimum wage for a woman. Back then minimum wage was lower for a woman than it was for a man. Then I'd make nine dollars or ten dollars a day, 'cause, see, I worked so hard that I always made over the production quota.

That first day, I went in and I was scared to death. I was so nervous. I felt like I couldn't do it, but then I knew I had to. Bar-tacking is sewing the seams in ladies' underwear. I'd turn the panties wrong side out and tack 'em up. If they were little girls' panties, I'd tack on little bows. Now they got the overlock machines and they don't need the bar-tackers. Chrissie Jane Hunt taught me my job. She had worked there for three or four years and she was the best one in there. I learned to work fast, real fast. If somebody came by to speak to me, it would take me a few minutes to get myself together to answer them back. When you go at something that hard, your mind gets idled and your head gets messed up. I could do good production but I could never work as fast as Chrissie Jane Hunt. You had to learn how to take shortcuts, hold your work in your lap and bring it up. You'd hold all you could in your lap because it saved time reaching up. You'd learn how to lay your garments just so, in order to get them stacked up right. That way you wouldn't have to waste time straightening them out. Little shortcuts like that.

They kept the production quota real high. If anybody made any money, what I mean is making over production, they'd send a quality control man around to time you. Then they'd up production and tell everybody else, listen, they doing such and such, so you got to do such and such. They made sure you didn't make more than a dollar or two over production. There wasn't that much to it, really, just a matter of speed, working real hard, and sticking with it. I had to stick with it because I needed the money, but oh God, did I hate it. The man I worked for there, the overseer, treated women bad, very, very bad, like they were stray dogs. I remember he was a red-headed man and he scared me to death. When he walked by my machine I'd just tremble.

I worked at the Carolina Underwear seven years. Then I got married and we moved to High Point where my husband worked as a fireman. I had another baby and went back to work at the Archdale Lingerie, which was only about two or three miles from where we lived. I really didn't like sewing but this place was close to home so I could walk to work and the pay was pretty good.

I worked there the whole time I lived with my husband, except when I was in the hospital from him beating me up. My husband wanted me to work and bring that check home. He also thought I should do all the housework, take care of the children, and take care of him. I'd work all day, come home and put out a wash, fix dinner, clean up the kitchen, get the kids' things ready for school the next day, get them to bed, and then sometimes I'd be up to three or four in the morning mopping floors and ironing. All he did was go to work, come home, and booze it up.

My husband always thought he was superior to me. His family wasn't really rich, but they seemed that way to me. They lived in the nicest section of Thomasville. They had raised tobacco all their lives, not big-time farmers, but they did good enough to buy into some real estate and turn a profit off of it when that land got developed. So they all lived in these fancy brick houses over near Erwin Park. All his sisters thought they were so much better than me and his mother hated me because I had had my first daughter before I was married and because I was from the mill hill. He didn't start beating me bad until we moved to High Point away from all my people. His mother had helped us build a little house, just a small four-room house, on a lot in a neighborhood of working people just like us.

Then he started drinking real bad, coming home after being in fights in the bar. After a while he started staying home, and at one point around 1962 I could count on getting beat up bad at least once a week. I ask God for forgiveness every day for what I put my children through during those years. He would get mad any time I showed any independence. Not that I did that often.

Most of the time we all did whatever he said and almost walked on our tiptoes when he was around. My oldest daughter was scared to speak around him. When he got mad he would beat me and tear up everything in the house. One night he beat me so bad that I was unconscious on the couch bleeding from the head. My oldest daughter, who was about nine then, ran across the street and called the police. When they got there she ran back and told them what had happened. I was unconscious and there was glass all over the floor. My husband told the police that he worked for the city and that I had slipped on a rug and hit my head. So they just left. They left me dying and my children at the mercy of that maniac. Well, she ran out and called an ambulance and I was in the hospital for weeks and weeks. That was the kind of hell I lived in for ten years. I did it because I thought that if my kids had a home and if my daughter had a last name like the rest of the family, we could be happy. I was so stupid. I was thinking about appearances, the way things looked to everybody else. He resented my daughter and called her ugly names like bastard. He had even less respect for me and called me whore and linthead.

I had always wanted to be a school teacher, but I quit school in 1949 in the tenth grade when I got pregnant. Neither one of my parents could read or write a word. Daddy worked at the Thomasville Furniture factory. Mama has worked in the Amazon Cotton Mill since she was ten years old. She's seventy-five now and she still works six nights a week. I remember when I was growing up I hated her working in that mill. There were five of us kids and she never had any time for us. If we asked her something she would say, "Leave me alone, I'm too tired." She was a hard-working woman who believed the wash was to be done on Monday, the ironing on Tuesday, and stuff like that. Both my mama and daddy worked hard, but we lived poor, poor, poor. We just had to do the best we could. My dad was a loving person, he always had time for us kids, and if one of us was sick he'd sit up with us to make sure we were all right. He was careless with money, though. If he had five dollars in his pocket, he'd spend it that day. It was up to my mother to make sure we had enough to eat in the house. He would drink and then him and Mama would get into it because she didn't believe in drinking. If she found his bottle she'd pour it out.

We lived on the edge of the Amazon Mill section, but we never lived in a mill house. My daddy would rent us a three-room house and paint that thing inside and out every year. Finally Daddy built us a three-room house on Trotter Street. Everybody in the neighborhood worked in the Amazon, and we were a typical mill family. Us kids would get out in the street and play ball. We weren't made to come in and do our homework because our parents didn't know the first thing about education. There were never any newspapers, magazines, or books in our house because Mama and Daddy couldn't read, but I would ask a neighbor for a newspaper sometimes and bring it home and read it.

When us kids would go out, we either went to the movies or to church. Sometimes the uptown boys would go out with mill workers' girls but they really didn't think these mill girls were good enough for them. That's what happened to me. I met this guy in church and I thought he really loved me. I think he did deep down inside but because I was from the mill section, he didn't think I was good enough for him. He was the son of the Methodist minister and he is the father of my first daughter. When I was dating him, well, when I say dating, Daddy wouldn't let me date anybody. He caught me and this guy at a friend's house one night and he said, "If you want to date her you come to the house and date her right."

So that Wednesday night he came to the house. I was reading the paper to Daddy. Daddy loved for me to read the Bible or the newspaper to him. Henry Ford had died that day, I never will forget it. Well, I asked Daddy if I could go with him and he said, "All right, but have her back home by ten o'clock." So we went out and he had me home by ten. Then on Saturday night he came by and asked me to start going with him. His father had died and I guess around this time his social standing was beginning to fall. His mother had had to go to work to support herself and her family. He was used to living in the church and in parsonages, but by then he was beginning to be known as a roughneck because he had started hanging out with the boys in my neighborhood and getting into trouble. I guess I trusted him because he was a minister's son, and I thought he was special. He thought he was pretty special too. When I told him I was pregnant, he just said that he had to finish getting his education and that he'd see me around. In other words, he didn't care what I planned to do.

Then Daddy died. Drunk, he and his uncle got in a fight over some moonshine they had been hauling, and Daddy got shot in the head. He was no more than buried when I found out that I was pregnant. Mama was at her wits' end and she beat the hell out of me when she found out. I left town and went to live with my older sister Magalene in Greensboro. I didn't go to his family because I figured that would just bring even more disgrace on the family than we had suffered. This was typical though. When I look back, a whole lot of girls I grew up with got pregnant by boys outside the mill village. The girl was usually so scared she let the boy off scot-free. In my case, I went out with this guy for a couple of years and he knew how much I loved him, so he knew that I would eventually give in. And I did. Of course we didn't date every weekend. He would go do his thing—he was seeing other mill girls at the time—and I'd wait for him to come back. So I listened to Mama and went to live with my sister in Greensboro. I was supposed to give my baby away, but when it came down to it, I couldn't do it. I brought my baby back to Thomasville and let people know it was none of their business where she had come from. That was between me and the Lord.

From then on, though, I was kind of a marked woman. I guess that's why I ended up with the kind of husband that I had. I didn't think I deserved better. He took my paycheck and mistreated me and my daughter too. I took that shit for ten years before I finally woke up.

After I left him, I felt like I had lost everything. I rented us a little old apartment and sat down in it and just cried and cried and cried. My daughters were nine and sixteen by then. I was thirty-three. Then I went to work for Burlington Industries. The sewing factories were up and down at the time. You'd work for three days and be off for two. I stayed at Burlington for about six years and at the same time I went down to the Amazon and got a second job on a different shift. I worked two jobs in order to get the money together for a down payment on a house. I wasn't getting any child support from my ex-husband, and of course I never got a penny from my older daughter's father.

My mother has worked in the Amazon all her life, since she was about ten, so as a child I went in and out of the Amazon to see her and I knew everybody that worked there because I grew up in the Amazon Mill village. When I worked there I ran winding machines. At the Amazon the spinners take the cotton and run it into thread and when it comes to the winding room the winders take the thread and wind it off onto two-pound cones. You get paid by the pound. They weigh it out and that's how you make your money. Then they send the two-pound cones out to the weaving room. The Amazon was just like any of the other mills. If you worked hard, you got paid your money. That's what it was all about. Making money. Burlington was about the same except you didn't get paid by the pound. You just tied your ends up when one cone was full and started another cone. If you kept all your ends tied up you turned out a whole lot of cones of thread. You never wanted your ends to run down, because you never knew when a counter was coming around. At the Amazon they paid you by the pound, but at Burlington you could work all night long and then the end counter came along and if your ends were down, you'd catch shit. I worked from three p.m. to eleven p.m. at Burlington and from midnight to eight a.m. at the Amazon. When I got off, I'd go home and take the children to school and then come home and go to bed around ten and get up around two.

At the time I didn't think my work was dangerous but looking back now I realize it was, breathing in all that lint. The department I worked in was not air-conditioned at all. The cotton and lint would blow everywhere and you would perspire something terrible, but you'd just go on, your hair would be wet and everything, and you'd just go on working like that. That was just a way of life. My mama had done it all her life, so I didn't think much about it. I just thought about making the money to get me a house and to raise my kids so they would never have to do the things I've done. I was just trying to make a better life for them. All the women there felt the same way.

People were always getting hurt in some way, you know, getting your hand hurt or mashing your fingers. I did that but nothing really bad. Like when you're doffing off, which is pulling off a cone, you might mash your finger or scrub your hand against something. The worst thing that ever happened to me was one night I was working and I just happened to look up and they had a sliding door and my best friend was sitting there, she was the one who carried the yarn to weigh it up. I looked up, just happened to, and I seen that huge door falling and I hollered. She jumped up and ran toward me because she thought I had hurt myself. And when she did, the door fell right where she had been. It was a huge old door and if it had fallen on her it would have crushed her sure as the world. That was like a nightmare. It was an old sliding door that moved on a track, and it was real old. When they slid it back it came off the track and just fell over.

At the time I worked in the mill, the sanitary conditions were pretty bad. Lint was everywhere and the frames were dirty and greasy. As long as the thread was clean, that's all they cared about. This was around 1965. They had sweepers all the time sweeping up the lint. They had to because they had so much lint flying around that, if they hadn't, you wouldn't have known where you were going. As far as fresh air, there wasn't any. We left the doors open at night hoping some night air would come through. That was the sliding door I was telling you about. We were trying to get some ventilation because it was so hot in there. When the thread came from the spinning room, it had a lot of lint on it and when you would rewind it, the lint would blow all up in your nose, your ears, and your eyes. I've gotten so much lint in my eyes that they've become infected. I wouldn't go to the doctor because I couldn't afford it. I'd just pull a gob of cotton out of my eye, put some eyedrops in it, and go on. After you worked in there a while you just got used to the lint. It would get all over your clothes. Before you went home you would take an air hose and blow off and then you'd go home and brush the rest off. So mill workers always left the mill with lint in their hair. That's why they were called lintheads. They had suctions that went around and vacuumed some of it up, but you'd still get a lot of lint on you. It was like a big hose about five inches' round and it goes on this conveyor belt on the ceiling. This thing goes up and down the aisles like an overhead vacuum cleaner with a huge hose hanging down. It's real light, so if it hits you it doesn't hurt. This thing vacuumed up what it could, but it couldn't get it all.

The mill smells like oil and grease because of the machines and of course the thread has an odor too. Early in the morning around four or five, when my stomach was weak, that smell would get to me. But I knew I had to do it. That was life. You wouldn't believe how noisy it is in there if you have never been in a mill. For years they never said anything about it, but then they went to giving you earplugs, which were awful to wear. They did that so you couldn't sue them if your hearing went bad, which is what happened to me. One of my ears, I can't hear out of at all. Everybody in my family has hearing problems because they have all worked in the cotton mill since they were kids.

Another thing was that there were always speed-ups. They'd come by and speed up your machines and they worked your tail off, because maybe they got this order that they needed to get out and you got to keep your ends tied up. Course we made more money that way if we could keep the machines up. They also had what is known as a stretch-out. I remember this one night in particular at the Amazon. I was running twenty-two sets of frames, which was a lot for the type of job I had. The lady across from me had stayed out of work that night and they needed those machines going. So this little strawboss (when I say strawboss I mean he was not much higher than me, I guess, but he was making a little more money), he was responsible for getting this order out. He said we needed to get all this woman's machines running and he did. I worked my fool self to death that night. We could never help each other out with our jobs because everybody had so much to do just to make it themselves. The men had jobs like strawbosses, overseers, supervisors, and the higher executive jobs. If a young boy come to the mill, he'd start out sweeping until he learned how everything was done and all, and then if he stayed there long enough he would get a position as a fixer, a doffer,* or as a strawboss, and could work his way up. They never gave a boss man's job to a woman. I resented that. I know I was smarter than a lot of them that I worked for.

The supervisors watched every move you made. That was their job, to walk around and watch you, see that you do your work right. That's all they would do was walk around. When I quit the Amazon, the man that was over me, the supervisor, said he wanted to see me. I had told the strawboss that I was leaving. I told the supervisor that I wasn't making enough money and I was going to work at Burlington Mills. They didn't know that I was already working there on another shift. I told him I could make more money at Burlington Mills because I could get better frames. I hadn't worked at the Amazon long enough to get good frames —the longer you're there, the better frames you got and the more money you could make. So he said if I stayed at the Amazon he'd give me this other lady's frames. She was in her fifties and had been working there much longer than me. I was in my thirties then so I said, "Yeah, and when I get in my fifties, you'll take my frames and give them to somebody thirty. No thanks." This woman was real nice and she worked as hard as I did. I thought since she had been there for all these years she deserved to keep her

---

*A fixer is a worker who repairs the
machines, and a doffer is a worker
who removes the spools from the
spinning machines when they are
full.

frames. I wanted to make as much money as her but I didn't want to take money away from anybody else to do it.

I don't think any of us needed all that supervision. I mean, if I was doing something wrong I wasn't too proud to be told, but as well as I knew my job and as hard as I worked, I really didn't appreciate somebody standing over me breathing down my neck. The supervisors would see women talking and they would go and tell them to get back to work. We were allowed to go to the bathroom but we had to run there and get right back. If you stayed too long, your machine would stop off* and then the boss man would really get you. That's why a whole lot of people who worked in the mill have trouble with their bowels, from having to hold them for eight hours. You tried to go to the bathroom before and after work. You really didn't have time to during work. Of course sometimes when nature called you had to go, but if it didn't call too bad you tried to wait. That became one of my biggest problems.

At lunchtime or dinner break, we had machines where you could get drinks and crackers and cakes, stuff like that. The machines were in a small room with carts and boxes, no tables or chairs. You sat on the boxes if you had time to sit down, but nobody did. You just had time to go get a drink and come back. You could take ten minutes for lunch. You'd go get your lunch and come on back to your machine and eat while you worked.

One time this supervisor put me on this bad set of machines and I complained because my threads kept breaking and that was the whole idea, tying up ends. The threads kept breaking and I was running to keep them tied up. I kept complaining to him that I couldn't make any money and he wouldn't do anything about it, so I just started tying them up the best I could to make the money. There are different kinds of knots and with this particular kind of job you weren't suppose to tie chicken-head knots, which was the fastest kind. But I said the heck with him, I'm going to tie chicken-heads because I got to make the money. Then he

---

* Shut down.

120

come and complained to me and we got into it about that. Well, there was more to the story than that. This particular boss man was going out with some of his workers. He had said something to me about going out with him and I had said no. He was married and I knew his wife. I used to work with her. Well after I had said no, he put me on this bad set of machines. One thing led to another and I quit.

When you have a grievance in the mill, you can do one of two things. You can go to your boss man and argue with him until he fires you, or you can go to another mill worker and complain to her and then forget it. However, the boss man favored some women over the others. He'd give the ones he liked the best set of machines. It was supposed to go according to seniority, but we all knew that it didn't always work that way. Management liked competition between us women because they wanted to get the most work done for the least amount of money. Money was the name of the game. Favoritism meant like, you go out with me and I'll see that you get a good set of machines and make good money. I never was a part of this. That was why I quit that time. Me and my boss had a big fight about it. I quit my job at four o'clock in the morning and went home. I was so mad I didn't realize what I had done until I got home. Then I decided that I wasn't going to let him get away with this, so I waited until after nine o'clock and went back to the mill to talk to someone in the personnel office, who, as it turned out, was also involved with going out with the women. I know that now, but at the time, when he told me, "I'll help you," I believed him. Well, he got me on at another plant and even got me first shift. I had been working third. Then the whole thing died down. His transferring me was just a cover-up, a hush-hush, because he was afraid I was going to tell the whole story.

Now that stuff is still going on today because I talk to the women still in there today and that's what they say. The boss men had a lot of control over your life. The ones they respected the least was the ones that didn't stand up for their rights. If you kept your mouth shut and just went on and did your job, then they'd do you around. But if you told them, "Listen, I'm not going to do this," then they'd give you a better job. Men were always superior over women. I guess that's the best way of describing it. The women had a choice; they could speak up for themselves and risk getting fired or play the game—the dating game.

I worked at that job for Burlington for a few more years and then they closed that plant down. They were running fiber glass drapes on one end of the mill and men's suits on the other, and the fiber glass from the drapes got into the men's suits. They closed the mill down and I got laid off. So I went back to restaurant work and got a job at Control Data collating computer cards. I worked both these jobs to be able to keep up with the bills. I liked the work and the people at Control Data. It was such a relief to be out of the mill. Then in 1971 my arm got caught in the machine and I haven't worked since.

About a year later I married again, this time to a boy who had grown up near me. All his people had worked in the mill. We had even dated when we were still teenagers. He had been living in Florida and when his wife passed away, he came back home. He called me up one day and a few months later we were married. At first we bought a beautiful brick home, but when it got to be too much work keeping it up, we sold it and took a cross-country trip before moving to St. Petersburg Beach, Florida, where we live now. I walk miles and miles on the beach every day.

Looking back, if I had to do it all over again, I would have tried to get some help. I wouldn't have been so stubborn and hard on myself. There were times when me and my kids didn't have enough to eat or a decent place to live, and I thought welfare and food stamps were too degrading. I never got any support from my ex-husband. I let my older daughter's father off scot-free. If I had it to do over again, I wouldn't be so proud.

BLACK WORKERS,
WHITE MILL TOWN

To help out with the housework and the caring for children, many mill women could afford to hire a black domestic whose wages were as low as pennies a day. She often lived in the mill family's home—sometimes sharing a bed with the children or sleeping in a makeshift bed in the hallway. Her rearing white children and maintaining homes in the mill village was an essential service that propped up the substructure of mill life, because it freed the white woman to sell her labor power in the mill.

This arrangement, which rendered the black woman virtually an indentured servant, also supported the goals of the original architects of the mill village system. Without the services that the southern black woman provided, that system would not have worked for most mill families. She was cook, housekeeper, and surrogate mother in a home where the real mother spent most of her time in the mill. It was her job to raise and maintain a family of potential mill workers even as she was not allowed to work in the mill herself. The difficulties that arose out of such a dynamic were many. For instance, it was not uncommon for white women to be jealous of the amount of time black women spent with their children in their homes. Meanwhile, the black woman would have to struggle with the fact that she had left her own children to fend for themselves while she went off to take care of white children.

The black woman was expected to marry, but the pressure to

do so was not as impending as it was for her white counterpart. For one thing, during the first half of the century young black girls were almost invariably hired out as domestics. Most often they went to live in the homes of their employers. This removed the burden of feeding at least one mouth in the family and made room in the tiny houses for the younger children. Marriage was also delayed in many cases because "there wasn't much to get married on." When the black woman did marry, she was also expected to work, but her economic position within her immediate family was somewhat different than that of her white counterpart.

As domestics in private homes, as well as in industry, black women had many more job opportunities than did black men. A black man might find a job as a janitor in a business that employed two hundred people, while each of those two hundred employees might hire a black woman to work in their homes. If she was willing and desperate enough to work for literally pennies per hour, the black woman could always find a job in a white woman's kitchen. As for the few black men who were hired by the mills before the 1960s, their work was limited to driving trucks, tending the grounds, and the heaviest or most hazardous jobs.

As in the white community, the measure of a man was dependent on his ability to provide for his family. The southern black man's inability to do so and his resulting frustration are not surprising. In many cases his frustrations led to a separation of ways between him and his family. But whether he left or not, often the black woman was the main provider and in many cases the sole support of her family.

Most southern black women remained in domestic work until the latter part of the century when southern industry finally opened its doors to them. Those few black women who found work in the mills in the early part of the century were hired in custodial positions. It was not until the sixties and the civil rights movement, some fifty years later, that black women worked alongside white women in the mills. When the mills began hiring black women, their starting salaries were often higher than those of the black men who had worked at these heavy and hazardous jobs for decades—and even then they were paid a wage lower than that of the white women who worked beside them at the same job.

SHELBY KIRK

Landis, North Carolina

I was born in 1894 and was named Shelby Daisy Estelle Grimm. That was my maiden name. I was born in Cabarrus County, and I had three brothers and sisters. There was seven of us. I was the third one. See, we farmed. I was raised on a farm. My daddy didn't own no land, he rented it. We grew cotton, corn, wheat, and oats, that's what we raised. See, he was a farmer. Oh yes, I worked in the fields, that's where I was raised at. I don't know how old I was when I went to work in the field, I just know our daddy put us in the field as soon as we could do something. I don't know how old I was then, I just remember I could walk. But he put us into the fields just as soon as we could do something, just as soon as we could hoe cotton or pick cotton.

Yeah, he put us in the fields. We lived way over there in the country, way over yonder on Coddle Creek. My daddy raised fifteen to twenty bales of cotton. We'd pick it, carry it to the gin to have it cleaned, then baled it and sold it. Oh yeah, I've picked a hundred pounds of cotton in a day. The first time I did, I remember my daddy told me that if I picked a hundred pounds of cotton that day, he'd give me fifty cents. I picked a hundred pounds of cotton that day and the next day I couldn't walk I was so sore. I was thirteen years old, that was my birthday, I never will forget it. I kept that fifty cents so long, I don't know what I did with it. I worked in the fields until I got a job in the mill. Then when I got a job in the mill, I still had a cotton patch at my daddy's. I'd go over there in the evenings and on Saturdays

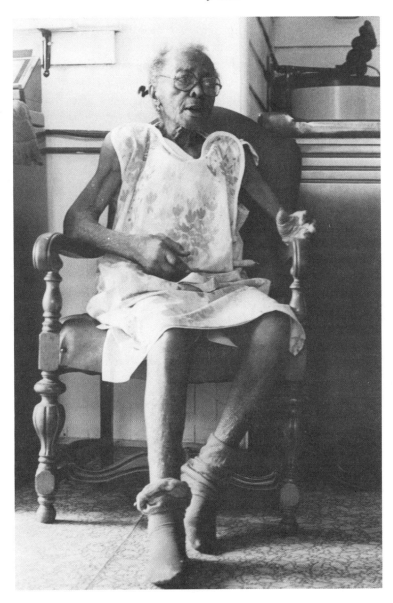

Shelby Kirk, 1984.
Photo by the author.

and pick cotton until I got all my cotton picking done. I had about four acres over there at my daddy's.

This man come down here one evening and said that a boss man in the cotton mill had told him to find four black women to work in the mill. So he came down here and asked me and three other women if we would go and try to work in the Collier Mill, and that's where we found a job. We was to clean up. Miss Ethel and myself was the first black women to work in the mill in Landis. I was a teenager by then, married and had two children.

ANNIE ADAMS

Danville, Virginia

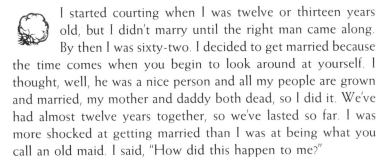 I started courting when I was twelve or thirteen years old, but I didn't marry until the right man came along. By then I was sixty-two. I decided to get married because the time comes when you begin to look around at yourself. I thought, well, he was a nice person and all my people are grown and married, my mother and daddy both dead, so I did it. We've had almost twelve years together, so we've lasted so far. I was more shocked at getting married than I was at being what you call an old maid. I said, "How did this happen to me?"

I remember seeing my grandparents only one time. See, they all left here to work in the Pennsylvania coke fields and the transportation was such that when they got in one place they stayed. My mama and daddy came back though, and they stayed here. Daddy had worked in the coke fields in Pennsylvania for four years and saved four hundred dollars for it. He was married then and Ella was the child they carried from Pennsylvania. I was the first one born after they came back, then my sister, America Breedlove, was born but she died. I was born not far from here in a cabin with three rooms. It had an upstairs and downstairs and the kitchen was on the back side as you came out the door. It had seven acres. We raised tobacco, corn, wheat, beans, and then all the vegetation we wanted to eat. We didn't buy anything, only coffee and sugar. We had a horse, a mule, hogs, and cows, and sometimes Daddy had extra meat to sell. We'd run a truck garden. Gather up the extra vegetables and then help Daddy peddle it in the street.

My mother was an active woman. She was always doing something in the church. She was a hard-working woman and a good neighbor. Doing something for somebody all the time. There were eleven of us kids and we would go to church and talk together. Sometimes we would ask her questions and she wouldn't answer right off. We'd ask such-and-such a thing and she'd say, "You'll learn." Yeah, my mama and daddy were hard-working people and number one they always taught us honesty. That is to do a job and to do it well. They were all into being honest. They just kept that before us. My daddy always taught us to respect people, all people. He would always tell us, "If you go right, people will follow you—seek out the right."

Mama taught us cleanliness. She was very strict on being clean. She cooked, cleaned up, raised eleven children, then sometimes the neighbors hired her by the day to do their wash. And in the fields, Mama was the main one. We children would do domestic work and when we did, we would live in with white folks and come home on weekends.

We didn't have the opportunity like the children do today to attend high school and go on to college and like that. And you would have to pay, even in the high school. We didn't have that kind of money, so when we finished elementary school that was it. Now, I went to the Ingleside Seminary. It was under the United Presbyterian Church for people who didn't have the money to do better. One year I worked in the laundry, one year I cleaned the teachers' rooms and consequently it didn't cost me too much. I wasn't missed at home, because those underneath me grew up and pushed the others out. I liked everything about school because I thought it would increase my efficiency to do what I wanted to do, which I thought was to be helping someone. Sometimes, I would listen to the newscast and I would think, "Oh my, if I knew all that I could understand the world better." See, knowledge is acquired and if you don't apply it, it soon goes away. We live to learn. I like to be affiliated with people who like to learn, but I just wish I could have done more, got out and experienced more of what was going on.

My first schoolhouse was on my daddy's farm. He gave an acre to the school board to use. He gave it to them because he didn't want the children to have to walk so far to school. My oldest sister and brother had to walk five miles to the nearest school. It was a one-teacher school. My teacher's name was Hattie Dallas Ringe. Of course, she didn't have, I say, a lot of high-powered education, but she had good common sense. I went to school there until I finished the seventh grade. The school got so crowded one time that she let me teach primary grades, you know, like ABCs and all.

Then I went to this mission school, the Ingleside Seminary. It was about sixty miles between here and Richmond. I decided to go there because my parents didn't have any money and that was the best I could do. I studied biology, science, algebra, English, did a lot of reading and book reports. My favorite book was *Silas Marner*. It was a story about this rich man who got this woman with child and she wasn't good enough for him. She started walking to his home where they were having this big feast and she got caught in a snow storm and didn't make it. She aimed to get there and tell him about his child. I didn't appreciate him because I thought that he did her wrong. I thought she should have just forgotten about him and went on about her business.

After I finished at Ingleside, I went to Tula, Virginia, and got a teacher's certificate. But I got so disgusted with the school where I taught that I quit. My pay was only forty dollars a month anyway. When I came back, I went to work for a woman keeping her house and she paid me nine dollars a week, only four dollars less a month.

Then I decided to go to work in the mill for more money and more time off. When you do domestic work, you have to work all weekends, Sundays and all. I went to work in the mill in 1942. I knew a lady, Mrs. White (she was from New York) that I used to work for. She had a lot of bearing and she wrote me a recommendation. There weren't many black women that worked in the mill back then. She sent this letter to the employment office and that's what got me my job. My first job in the mill was just dealing with the waste. World War II broke out and took a lot of the men away from here and that gave us a break. And they started salvaging all the paper and strings and rags. They needed someone to take care of that, so that's what I did. The sweepers would sweep it up and I would shake it out and bag it. At the office, they'd have papers, a lot of papers, and they'd even salvage the lunch bags. I'd tear those open, shake all the leftover food out and collect those. That's what I did. I did it for about a year.

Then I helped sweep, and then they had cloth that ran from the machines to boxes, and I'd push those boxes of cloth to and from the machines, and clean and scrub the machinery. I did that for a long time. All the ends of the cloth that they would pick out from the weave room they'd bring it up, and I'd separate it and get it ready to ship out. Did that a long time. I'd mark them thin or heavy, some clean or dirty, some color or white. I'd separate them and get them in the boxes. They come off the machine and the inspectors, who be inspecting the cloth, and the bad places, they'd cut them out. That's what I was doing when I retired. I was the only one doing this kind of work. I worked on the first shift in the inspection room. The white women inspected the cloth. For a long time I was the only black woman that worked there. I didn't feel too badly about that, after all, I was used to it. After we leave our own family we just be around where another white go. It wasn't too hard, 'cause I had done it all my life. But then around 1962, the time of the civil rights movement, things started to change.

When I first went into the mill we had segregated water fountains. You know, one water fountain and over the top it said, "White" and we weren't allowed to go there, or we'd get fired for just drinking out of that fountain. Same thing about the toilets. I had to clean the toilets for the inspection room and then, when I got ready to go to the bathroom, I had to go all the way to the bottom of the stairs to the cellar. So I asked my boss man, "What's the difference? If I can go in there and clean them toilets, why can't I use them?" Finally, I started to use that toilet. I decided I wasn't going to walk a mile to go to the bathroom. If you let

Annie Adams

Annie Adams, 1984.
Photo by the author.

people know sometimes that you're not afraid, it helps a lot. That's how I survived in the mill.

One particular day, it was about three o'clock, we left at four, and you were supposed to leave your job clean. This foreman came up to me and told me to go out to the store and have this order filled. But I told him, "Naw, I don't have time to go, because if the boss were to come in here and find the floor dirty you could tell him that I didn't do my job." So he said, "You do what I say or punch the time clock out." And I said, "Naw, I'm going to stay here and do my job. You punch my time out." Well, he didn't do nothing. I didn't have too many problems because I would speak out, see. It's mighty hard for a person to drag you down when they know you're right.

You know, I could have inspected cloth. I always had this feeling that anything anybody else could do, I could do if I had a chance. But that chance didn't come until the sixties and by then I was getting ready to retire. When the civil rights movement began, I just looked at it as something that *had* to come. I was for anything that was right and the color of a person's skin doesn't mean a thing to me. The word that we need to go by is God's holy word and he said, "Love your neighbor as you love yourself." The color of a person's skin doesn't make him anything less than human. We had a right and all we needed was a chance. That's the way I feel, if you got the chance you can get out there and make it. Martin Luther King was a wonderful speaker. He said many things I had been thinking about. He was a sincere leader and he didn't believe in violence. A lot of the violence was against his wishes, because we can stand and reason things out without fighting, especially when you can see the wrong in it. That's how I feel about the civil rights movement: anything you get you gonna have to work and suffer for it. I look for things to get better yet, because it finally gonna get to the place where we will all be one people. When they took that sign down off the water fountain, I remember thinking, "Well, that's one step." I mean, what they thinking—that I'm gonna stand here and drink from one fountain and you gonna stand there and drink from another just because of the color of our skin? That's just simple-minded.

JOHNNY MAE FIELDS*

Kannapolis, North Carolina

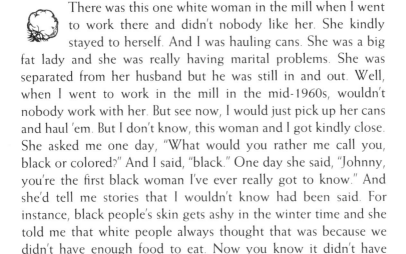There was this one white woman in the mill when I went to work there and didn't nobody like her. She kindly stayed to herself. And I was hauling cans. She was a big fat lady and she was really having marital problems. She was separated from her husband but he was still in and out. Well, when I went to work in the mill in the mid-1960s, wouldn't nobody work with her. But see now, I would just pick up her cans and haul 'em. But I don't know, this woman and I got kindly close. She asked me one day, "What would you rather me call you, black or colored?" And I said, "black." One day she said, "Johnny, you're the first black woman I've ever really got to know." And she'd tell me stories that I wouldn't know had been said. For instance, black people's skin gets ashy in the winter time and she told me that white people always thought that was because we didn't have enough food to eat. Now you know it didn't have nothing to do with that. So there was all these tales and we'd sit in the bathroom and she'd tell 'em to me and we'd laugh.

Now she had never liked black people, I knew that, I knew that when I was hauling her cans, that she didn't particularly like black people. But this woman fell in love with me. She really loved me and she's told people that she had never met anybody quite like me. I was used to talking to white people. You know, if you like people, you can talk to all people. There is no color line. Mama brought us up so we could talk to all people. So I

* Pseudonym.

137

got along, though there was some that didn't like me, and some that would make snide remarks.

One of the things that the mill did was give me an opportunity to do some things I wouldn't have been able to do. While we don't make that much money, it gave me an opportunity to make more money than doing anything else in Kannapolis. It gave me a chance to give my kids a college education. They couldn't have gone to school if I'd still be working in that cafeteria. I got along with every boss man that I had, some of them I didn't know their names but they knew mine. I always did my job. I'm the kind of person that has to do their job well. But I rarely had any problems. Now I could have had. It was there in the making if I had let it affect me. What I did was sometimes I would meet it head on and sometimes I would ignore it, whatever the situation called for. I've found that once you let a person know where you stand, I find that you get along with that person.

There was this one man in there and you know he was mean. So one day I just had a talk with him. We just talked. You know he didn't want to speak to me. He would try not to speak to me. But when he came in that door I'd say, "Hey Charlie, how you doing?" Then one of my girls broke her glasses in school, so Charlie was my foreman and I had asked off to go get her glasses fixed and he made the remark that I must not have been doing what I ought to, anybody break their glasses and not have another pair. So I said, "Charlie, now I'm not making the salary you make or she would have two pair of glasses." I didn't mention how she was doing in school, but the next week when her report card came out I took it in and laid it in his hand. And it wasn't nothing but A's. I never had to say another word to him about it. A lot of them didn't know I had eight children.

But I got along with them. I've had problems with some of them but you know the problems are always there. I've always asked God to give me wisdom to deal with them. Now this woman I was talking about, she was as mean as she could be and she was as greedy as she could be. And if it had been anybody but me they would have been fighting 'cause she would come over there on my job and get my cards. Now sometimes I would just bust out laughing, I'd get tickled at her and people would say, "Johnny why you laughing?" But I don't know, sometimes I would get tickled at her. And she would get so ashamed, she wouldn't do it no more.

Things don't make me mad so easy but I can get mad. But I don't get mad easy. People at the back would be getting mad, I mean white folks would be getting mad at her about coming over there and getting my cards, but I knew they was goin' to pay me my average if I ain't got no cotton. So why am I going to get so upset if she coming over there and getting the cotton? They never could seem to see that. They'd get mad because they felt like I was being taken advantage of, but I didn't care, I'd get tickled and I'd go in the bathroom and sit down and they'd come, these white women, and they'd say, "Johnny, don't worry, you ain't gonna lose any money." See if I had a choice, I wouldn't have done all that I've had to do, I would have chose to be a bit lazy. So when she come taking the cotton, I be hoping she take all of it. And the rest of them would be getting so mad.

I've got along, but now I haven't always been done right. You know, sometimes they don't know the meaning of fair. And that was definitely because I was black. If there are two jobs and one is just a little bit better the white woman will get the better job. No matter how qualified that black woman is, that's just the way it is. It's like that in the mill now. Some of 'em don't know the meaning of fairness. I have told them about it. The rest of the time I've been frustrated, like all people sometimes, and get over it and go on. 'Cause life don't stop. I've worked in the mill now for seventeen years and I think I've really got upset three times. Really hard down.

Like we got this white woman in the back and she's really lazy. Now what she does really affects my job. So we were really getting all the bad cotton. Okay. Now my boss man at the time, he liked people, he really did. But somehow they feel like they got to favor these white women. So I asked him when we didn't have no more cotton, I said, "Let me do something else." So what he

139

did was, he didn't stop me off.* But later on this white woman started complaining and he stopped her off. Now that made me mad. See now, I had asked him and I was having as hard a time as this white woman with this cotton, but he wouldn't stop me off. So she didn't do nothing else for the rest of the night. And I was getting all this bad cotton. And the more I thought about that, the madder I got. This is what I do with it sometimes, I don't often do this. I got my hat and coat and I was going to walk out the door. Then, "Johnny, come here, where you going?" This other boss man said, "Come on up in my office." So I went up there and said, "Mr. Griffin, I don't fuss about my work, I don't fuss about the cotton, and I don't, you know, when the rest of the people up in the office are fussing about the cotton and they job, I don't do that." I said, "You know I don't fuss about my job," and he said, "Yeah, I know that." And I said, "Well, I'm mad," I said, "You know my boss man likes those little girls back there and they don't tie up no ends." My boss man he said, "Don't they tie up ends?" And I answered, "I said they didn't." The other boss man said, "Well, Bud (that was my boss man) said. . . ." I said, "Bud don't run that job, I run that job, and I said they don't tie up no ends. I don't have to lie to you. They don't tie up no ends." Then they didn't say no more, because I guess they know when I come to 'em that I got a legitimate beef because I don't come to them that much.

Now I didn't blame that white woman because I couldn't blame her. It wasn't her fault. Now I wasn't going to get into it with her like what happens with other people 'cause it wasn't on her. It was on the boss man. So this boss man came down there and told her she had to tie up her ends or go home. She didn't get mad, but if she had, it would have made no difference to me. See she always got all the good cotton. Really, all the good cotton come from off her side. Now, by rights, they could have put the good cotton on one of my jobs. My job never runs as good as her side. Usually what happens is all the good cotton comes over

---

*Shut down the machine.

on her side. So this is what happens. And I really have to be talking to myself and praying and this is how I have to handle it. One day I asked, "I wonder why one side runs better than the other all the time?" I said, "If I was a boss man, it seems to me I'd be looking into that." I told them all that that day I was mad. I said, "I get all the bad cotton. All the good cotton goes to this job over here." But I didn't blame this white woman for that, it wasn't her fault, but there's a lot of things that go on that's not fair. The black woman don't have nobody to look after her in the mill. Really, seem like the white men in the mill look after the white women, and the black men look after the white women, and seem like the black women ain't got nobody to look after them but theyselves.

I try not to let it get to me. 'Cause you know I use this philosophy. I say to myself, well I'm here for eight hours and then I'm goin' on home and the rest of the time is on my own. My mother always told me, "If the white woman want salt in her pie, put salt in her pie." So that's what I do. If they tell me something and I know I ain't going to do it, I don't tell them, I just go on and don't do it. For instance my boss man was telling me to do all this off-the-wall stuff and I told him, I said, "Stop telling me to do all this off-the-wall stuff." I had come to the first shift temporarily and I didn't have no job so they had all these old odd jobs that was really men's work and he'd just walk up to me and ask me to do them. Now there was this other white woman there that didn't have no job either, but he never asked her to do these odd jobs. For instance, I was pushing cans and he would never let her push cans. Now pushing cans was hard. What he would have her do was clean out boxes, pick the paper or cotton out of the box or something. See now she loved me and I loved her to death, but see now that wasn't fair. So one day I just told him to stop asking me to do these odd jobs—off-the-wall jobs is what I called them. And he said, "Johnny, you the only one ain't got no job." So I said, "Just tell me to go home, I got a home to go to and it's mine." After that he never did ask me to do that again—never did tell me to go home—but he never asked me to do those jobs again.

One time they was building something and my boss man asked me, he said, "Johnny, will you get those planks back there and move them?" And I said, "If I get to it." Now I knew I wasn't going to get to it and I think he knew I wasn't going to get to it. Now some of them would say, "No, I ain't doing such-and-such a thing, I'm not going to do that." I never did that. I'd say, "Yeah I'll be glad to, if I get to it." He knew I wasn't going to get to it, you see. 'Cause he would look at me and grin. That's the way I learned to handle it.

Now one time I refused to do my job. I told you this one white woman I worked with was greedy. I was hauling cans at that time and this woman came over there and picked up another drum and that means that I got all these extra cans to haul. She didn't have to pick up that drum. I told 'em, "I ain't haulin' them cans." What happened was I was a drawing hand and they closed down my job. They don't have that job now. And at that time I was making top dollar 'cause I was good at my job, and I had had a good week. Then something had happened to my drawings and it was going to be closed for something like six to eight weeks. So whatever job I had they had to pay me that top dollar salary. Okay, so I had this job haulin' cans which paid three dollars an hour but they had to pay me six dollars an hour. So they want me to work for it and bring up all these drums. And I was tired, my feets was tired and sore from walking across the steel thing on the floor, and I said, "I'm not hauling them. Now she can run them if she wants to but I'm not hauling them." So these cans got way out in the floor, all these cans sitting out there. So my boss man went up there and got the big boss man and said, "Johnny won't haul all these cans." Yeah, I went in the bathroom and sit down. They would have probably fired me that day but you know what happened. All the black women hauled all those cans away to keep me from getting fired. I don't know, they just helped me like that. Rather than let them fire me, they hauled them cans.

CORINE LYTLE CANNON

Kannapolis, North Carolina

I was born December 1, 1919. My family had just a little more than most of the families that lived around us, 'cause Papa was so energetic. In the church his name is on the cornerstone and he was the secretary of the church. I can remember my daddy had a truck and my uncle had a truck and my brother and one of the hired hands, they would sneak a ride into South Carolina and hide themselves around that night, then they'd load people up on those trucks, put as many people on that truck as they could, and in the middle of the night they would bring them out of South Carolina. They did that because it was so hard for people to make a living down there. They'd bring them up here in North Carolina to the chicken farms. See, my grandmother raised them up through slavery. So they'd go down to South Carolina and bring these people up here where they could make a good living.

I don't remember us having a whole lot of racial problems. I didn't know until I was grown and come to this area that people hated me. See, you don't know you down until somebody drag you down or put you down. The first time I felt like I was looked down on—I've told this so many times now—my daughter in her thirties now, well when she got sick, she was about five or six years old. It was real hot one day and we were sitting out on the front porch, and she blacked out. It scared me real bad and I carried her to the hospital and they said she was overcome with heat. About two or three months after that she had another spell like that. I carried her to the hospital again and got another doctor and he said he thought she was probably suffering from epilepsy. So he made an appointment for me to go to Winston to the hospital up there for her to have some tests. I was supposed to hear from him the next week and that week I didn't hear from him. The next week I inquired and I still didn't hear anything and about the third week I went down to talk to the doctor. So I went in his office and he said, "I really hate to tell you this, but I can't get your daughter into the hospital because she's colored,"—(we were "colored" then)— "and they won't take colored there. Now Corine, I'm working on it. I really feel bad about it and the reason I haven't got back to you about it is that I'm seeing if I can get her in somewhere else."

So he did. In about a week he called back and said he got her in at Chapel Hill. So we all went down there. We were all so excited to go so far, so we all loaded up the station wagon. We left early that morning, oh about five-thirty so we'd be there early. Carried food and everything. So we got there and I don't think they opened up until about seven-thirty and we was already there. I went in to talk to them about it and they asked, "Well, how many is in your family?" And I told them. Then they wanted to know how did we sleep. So I said, "Everybody in my house sleeps separately by themselves except me and my husband," 'cause I had two sets of bunk beds and the baby slept in the baby bed. Then they asked, "Who all works?" So I asked, "Well what do you mean?" And they said, "Well, how else you gonna pay for this?" So I said that my husband and I worked. And they asked, "How do you manage?" Well, here I was thinking that I was very well off. See, they was doing this to see how much we were required to pay. So finally she said, "You pay a dollar for registration and pay for all your medicine and all the rest is free." That's the first time I remember our family ever getting anything. There was twenty of us kids, but I never remember us getting any welfare.

Our mother always instilled it into us and, I don't know, sometimes when I'm talking to my children I think it might have been a little too strong, but my mama always said, "Now when you doing something, try to do it just a little bit better than anybody else." My mama always taught that to us.

We were taught to win and we thought of ourselves as winners. We were the first, the best. We're not very good losers. One time my daughter was in the spelling bee and I told her, "If you lose, don't cry. Just do the best you can do." So she went on and later I got this telephone call and she was just a crying. I said, "I told you not to cry," and she said, "You said if I lose don't cry."

My mother was a brilliant person. She came second to nobody. She gave up going to Barber Scotia so her sister could go. So she was what you call a self-educated person. Any subject you could bring up my mama could talk about. She read and she could talk about anything. All the older children finished school and she could talk to them on anything that come up. She attended extension courses at A&T and the farmer's conferences and all such as that she was into.

She was very strict. You had to work, you had to be clean, and you had to look the part. Now you see pictures of black people out in the field. Well, let me tell you, Mama never went out into the field without first putting cold cream on her face, and she put stockings on her arms so she wouldn't get all messed up by the sun. She had beautiful long hair. It was long and she'd take that hair and she'd fix it up on her head. She'd go to Ivy's, you know, the most expensive store in town—Ivy's was the big one back then—and she'd go look at all the dresses and suits and things and she would go to the store and get her some material. She'd say, "Oh I'm going to the remnant counter," and she'd go to the remnant counter and she'd get her what she needed. Then she'd make her anything she saw just about.

When I come along the older ones was all gone and Papa was depressed because he had lost a lot of property during the Depression. It was taken from him. He had a nervous breakdown from it. He really got down. But Mama was his strength, she was the rock of the family. She would never, never, never give up. She would always say, "Well it could be worse. Let's get over this hurdle because there's another one coming." And "With this next one let's jump a little higher." And, "We can make do." And, "We'll just have to do like the people over the river, when we don't have it, we'll just have to do without it." And, "Wherever there's a will, there's a way." And "Whatever you do, do it just a little bit better than everybody else."

It would make us all strive so hard. It was hard for me to master long division and, you know, you'd have to go to the blackboard back then, and I'd always have family as teachers. My sister Kate and me were the youngest and we were really spoiled children 'cause we really did get a few things the other children didn't get. And I couldn't do long division. This cousin that was very close to me, I thought she was very pretty. She was very fair complexioned. She was pretty and I wasn't. I didn't know at the time that she could work long division. We were at the board and I had mine wrong and when the teacher told me I had mine wrong, my cousin laughed and I just jumped on her. I just jumped on her and everybody was wanting to know what's wrong. But that "do just a little bit better than everybody else" stuff was in me 'til, I don't know, when I couldn't get my way I'd hit you. Then there I was in front of the class and I felt so bad. I thought, "I know they gonna tell Mama." I got punished in school and then when I got home what Mama would do was sit you down and talk to you. I told her, "Mama, I don't know why I did it. When she laughed I just hit her." And she said, "Now baby, you mustn't do that. You're just as good as anybody else. You're just as good as any child God made." And she'd say, "Maybe you can't do that as good but you can do something else better."

My first work was when I was fourteen. The lady, who is my sister-in-law now but I had no idea about that at the time, she worked down in Kannapolis for some people and I went down there with her and she got me this job. I had never worked in the house but I could hoe as much cotton as anybody else my age. I could pick cotton, I could milk the cows, I could feed the horses, ride horseback, I could hitch up the plow. I could do whatever was being done 'cause I had never been in the house that much. But I got this job and it was for a white family that worked in the mill and I really didn't know how to do it. I could cook some because I'd been cooking a little. But Etta MacIntyre, that's who got me the job, told me, "Well, you do this first and then you do othern." I didn't make out too good on that job. Housework was not for me. I worked at a photo studio and I liked that, I worked at the laundry and I liked that, but I've always been a salesperson. I always had something to sell. But this cleaning job I think I got two dollars for the week. That must have been about 1934. Everybody was trying to teach and we only had a little old country school, so you could teach, or nurse, work in the hospital, or some of 'em made as much as fifteen dollars a week in the laundry, and that was real good money. Then you could work in the homes.

Back then most everybody slept in. I slept in then. I'd sleep in the kitchen or in the hallway or something. I made two dollars a week and I really don't know how much this woman I was working for made at the mill. That was something they always tried to keep a secret from us. But they were poor. They were poor financially.

I had a lot of different jobs. I married, see, when I was eighteen and after that I worked at this photo studio for about eighteen months, I guess. Then after we got in this house, I was about twenty, I worked at about two or three different laundries. I worked in the schools in the kitchens and then I worked at Woolworth's dime store. I opened it up and lit the stove, and I worked in the kitchen there for about two years. I quit there to have a baby and my friend took my place until I could come back. That was our understanding, but she retired from there. She worked there twenty years. My husband didn't want me to go back to work after I had my baby. He didn't want me to do nothing that would have me tied down, because he said the children wasn't going to be little but one time and if I worked I would have to leave them with other people and all like that.

So he was working on two jobs and I was selling. During World War II you couldn't get nylon hose. So there was a company out of Charlotte and they sent someone out to talk to the superin-

Corine Lytle Cannon on the day of her marriage.
Photo courtesy of Corine Lytle Cannon.

tendent of schools and he told the teachers and professional
people about how they could sell hose for one dollar a pair. So
I think Mrs. Willis ordered some and she told me about it and
asked, "Would you like to help?" And I said, "Yeah." Well this
man was named George and I don't know if his last name was
George or his first. I never called him nothing but George. He
was a white guy out of Charlotte. He used to come and bring
me stockings once a month. And I would get a hundred pair and
sell them for one dollar a pair. This was during World War II.
So I got to where I was selling three, four hundred pairs of
stockings a month. I made thirty-five cents on each pair.

Then I sold Stanley products. I'd have Stanley parties down
here from the Yadkin River down here to the Catawba. And I'd
average about a hundred dollars a party. I stopped that in about
1949 because my children was coming along and I'd have to have
parties at night and it got to be too much on me. I always did
my parties like a social. I'd invite the whole families, the men and
all. My parties would start at seven o'clock and we'd play games
and I'd entertain them until about eight or eight-thirty. I'd have
all types of entertainment, we'd play Bingo and stuff like that,
and I'd act like a comedian. I could really do it. Like one time
this elderly man, Mr. Bill, I'd give him a bath brush and he'd take
his shoes off and get on the couch and show people how to take
a bath and he'd just throw up his legs and rub everywhere saying,
"Now you always rub up your legs to keep your nerves going so
you won't have shingles and things." And we'd have so much fun.
Yeah, I'd have a house full of people. Now I'm an Avon repre-
sentative and have been for quite some time. I have around thirty
people in my group and we are A-number one in our district. I
got my award last week and on the twenty-first we will be treated
for lunch at the K&W Cafeteria. So I said, "Yes Mama, I'm still
number one."

I went to work in the mill in 1962. I was the first black woman
hired. Jerry was my baby then. At that time what I was doing
was working at a dressing plant, and what we did there was dress
chickens, two and three days a week. Then I had heard that black

people were going to be allowed to go to sign up for work in the mill. I had gone to get my hair done and they were talking about it at the beauty shop and they were whispering, "Don't you know, so-and-so boss man told so-and-so to go down to the mill to sign up for work." So I went back to work that Monday and told everybody. So when we got off work we all went over to the mill, and we all walked in. So I walked up to the desk and asked if it was possible for us to sign up for work, and they said yes. So we all signed up. All women. Then we all went back. We all said, "Don't tell nobody, don't tell nobody." We just wanted to see what the outcome would be. We whispered it, you know, there was some things that you just didn't talk about. It was just a new area that was opening up for blacks and you just didn't talk about it.

So I had already planned to tell them that I was going to work a production job. I told them that I wasn't going to lift a broom. I told them that when I signed up. I said, "Y'all can get all the janitorial jobs that you want, but I'm not a servant and I'm not going to lift a broom." So back at work we made a lot of jokes about it. Well, I went to work on Monday and come Tuesday I told them I wasn't going to work that day. I have something like ESP, you know, something that tells you when something is going to happen. I can just about tell when something is going to happen. So I told them I wasn't going to work today because I told them that I imagined my letter was coming to tell me to go to work in the mill. So they just laughed and went on. So after work they came by and came in and I was in there on the couch. And they said, "You haven't got your letter yet," and I said, "No," and I was so disappointed that I hadn't got a card saying, "Yeah, come on in." And they just laughed. Just about that time the telephone rang. And I answered it, said, "Hello," and they said, "This is Cannon Mills calling, does Corine Cannon live there?" and I said, "Yes she does." "Well, we want to know if you can come to work in the morning, come over to the office in the morning at eight o'clock." And I said, "Yes, I'm sure I can." And they said, "Come prepared. We might need you to work." I said,

"Well good." And these girls in there laughing, they just came to tease me for missing a day of work up there. So the man said, "Do you know Mary Harris?" I said, "Know who?" "Mary Harris." I said, "Where does she live?" "On Long Street." That was Long Street then. "From the address I believe she lives near you." I said, "Oh, is it Mary Lee Harris?" "Yeah, could you get in touch with her for us? She doesn't have a telephone. Bring her with you." I said, "I sure will." I hung up and just jumped up and shouted. "I told you, I knew it, I got up this morning and I had that feeling." I said, "Y'all stay right here." And I ran out of the house and up the street and said, "Mary Lee." She said, "What?" "They said for us to come to work in the morning at Cannon Mills." Mary Lee started screaming "Heeeeey!" and I came running back down here.

So that next morning me and Mary Lee walked into the superintendent's office. "Good morning, come right on in." He had us to sit down. Then he said, "This is something new and I have to admit I feel like it should have been done earlier, but this is the way it is." He said, "I'll tell you, you'll be an example. Everybody is going to look at you." He said, "But if anybody looks at you scornful or says anything unpleasant, please don't answer back, please don't answer back. First get the name and where they work and please tell me." And he said, "You were chosen, Cannon Mills have seen so many black people and you were chosen." And all this time he was standing with his back to us. He got up from the desk and turned his back to us and said, "This is new and try to make the best of it. You have been chosen and you are going to be an example." And he stood like this with his back to us, looking out the window. I think he thought his face was going to be red because you could tell from the back that his ears and his neck were turning red. You really could.

Now I've always been very assertive and I could always just say what I wanted to. So I asked questions. "Just what type work is it going to be?" 'Cause I was going to say right then that I was not sweeping and I was not going there to be any different than anybody else. Nothing from nothing leaves nothing so I had nothing to lose. So I had my little speech made. I was going to work on the same level as everybody else. There was this one girl who had called herself my friend and she worked in the sewing room. She had said, "I'll be so glad if they hire you, I'll be so happy 'cause it's past time for you to be there. Maybe you'll get a chance to be the janitor in my department." I said, "Rachel, what you talking about? You better be quiet, I might take your job." And we just laughed and I knew that she was thinking that I was going to come in there to do cleaning. But I said, "No, uh-uh." I said, "What you doing?" And she said, "Hemming sheets." So I said, "Well, if they don't have two machines for that you gonna have to get up." And she would look so funny when I would say things like that 'cause, see, I would work for her some during the week. I did day work.

So anyway, they took us down and showed us our job. They had opened up a whole new department. There wasn't anything in it. It was just a warehouse. They had put the cocker warpers in there.* This is a big machine and you put the cheese of yarn, these big spools of yarn that they called cheeses, up on there, run it up and it runs up to the big beams and you run this yarn off. This yarn goes from there to the weave room. It comes out of the spinning room where the yarn is wound. They open up the cotton and it goes in there and it goes into what is called roping. We call it roping 'cause it looks like a rope and then it goes to the spinning room in big old cans and then the yarn comes to us in thread and then it's run through the machine and then it's slashed and starched and then goes to the weave room and gets made into cloth.

So they showed us how to do it. They took us out to a brand new place, a warehouse that they had opened up just for us. See, they didn't know what the racial tension was going to be. They had us in there with one white woman. She was very nice, she was a Christian woman from the Baptist church. We both were Presbyterian so we talked church a lot. And then we had this one

---

*A cocker warper is a machine that
twists yarn to arrange it for weaving.

white man that doffed the beams for us. So it was just us two black women, one white woman, and this white man. We would have to go out to the canteen to get our drinks and things and people would stare and turn around and look at us like they thought we weren't supposed to be there. And I reckon we felt like we were being watched. Mama had taught me that we were as good as anybody else, so we would go to the mill very neatly dressed up at first, but then we found that it would be easier for us to wear pants or jeans. Then we worked about a week or ten days and they hired four more black women. Two for the second shift and two for the third shift. And they put them in the same department. And we six black women worked there for about eighteen months before they hired any more black women. On the second shift they had a white woman working in there and on the third they had a white woman. Then in '65 they just flooded the place with black women.

But it was really a trial thing when we first went in there. There was Mary Lee Harris and myself on the first, Lorine Cowry and Katie McErie on the second, Dorothy Forrester and Earline Alexander on the third. Everybody was extremely nice to us. We worked there for about a year hourly and then they started bringing other black people in. Black women from everywhere, I didn't know there were so many black women. Then they started letting us bring students in. You know, students would work in the afternoon for a while. And it got to be just a real good thing. And people accepted us. Very few things happened racially. We were hired at first on an hourly basis. I was making $1.35 an hour. I don't know what the white woman was making. You know, that was always a big secret. And you weren't supposed to tell anybody what you made.

You know my husband Esau had worked at the mill driving a truck all his life and I started out making more than he did. I think he was making about $1.30 an hour, and I was making $1.35 an hour. So the Legal Aid of the NAACP made a suit against Cannon Mills. A lot of black people got money out of that suit. I didn't get any money because I didn't work long before they put me on production. I told them, "I'm not going to work if I have to work hourly, I'm not going to sweep, I'm not going to lift a broom." I'm not going to do that, I made it plain.

But see, when they made that suit, Ralph Nader was here. They stopped out in front of my house, Ralph Nader's group. The girl that was working with him was active in the NAACP and was very fair. She was about the complexion of a white person. She wore her hair parted and she looked like she could have been your relative. She had worked a lot with integrating housing in Charlotte. She would apply for an apartment and when she wouldn't get it the NAACP would sue. See, she was set up like that to integrate the housing. Then she went with another group and they didn't know she was black. They were all working in housing development and she got a job there. And so that night she opened up the conversation saying how she hoped they wouldn't let any black people in, because she said she didn't think it was right, that they shouldn't be bothered. Oh she really put on. She said this while they were all out eating one night. She opened up the conversation saying that she hoped they didn't let blacks into these housing developments. "We don't need them," she said. When she said that, naturally people just opened up and went to talking. She said, "You know, these black people who are applying for these houses and apartments and things, I hope they don't get them because we don't need them in there." And that's all she had to say because then they said, "I'm with you, 'cause you know. . . ." And they just opened up and started talking about how awful black people were. And this woman would get all the information that she needed for Ralph Nader's group to sue.

And they came right here to my house. It was about 1968 when the suit was. My daughter had a scholarship to go to college and my other daughters who were in college worked part time so that they could have the money to go to college. If they didn't have a whole lot to study, they would work five nights. One of my daughters was the first black student to get a scholarship from Cannon Mills and the other one was the first to work part-time like that. Now 1968 was the time of the civil rights movement.

Around here there was nothing happening really. See, Cannon owned the whole town. All the schools are on Cannon property, all the churches are on Cannon property. See, because they owned the property, when Mr. Cannon or the board of directors decided to do something, that's the way you had to do it. There were no demonstrations in Kannapolis. The first sit-ins were over there at Woolworth's in Greensboro, a boy out here was one of them. But his daddy is still working in the mill so we don't tell that. We whispered such as that. We whispered it. As a race, you definitely don't tell white people your business. You definitely don't do that. You only talk to the ones that, well, if they don't got nothing to give you, you don't tell them nothing. See, if a white woman comes up to give you a ride, she doesn't come into your house. But I know exactly what the menu is in her house— what they eat and what they don't like. I know how they dress, what kind of clothes they have, because I've worked in their houses. They don't know what goes on in our part of town but we see what goes on in theirs. Who goes with who, and they do a lot of that. This man goes with this one and all that. But white people don't know that about us. So that's why we were taught always to keep these things secret.

But anyway, getting back to when the suit came up, they came up to my house and asked me if I would talk to anybody. I said, "Well, I'd rather not." I didn't push for that. Everybody was so surprised that I didn't take the lead. This same woman I was telling you about, well I'm like her aunt. They came out there and the car was from Georgia. I met them at the door and I said I'd rather not. They wanted to come in and talk to me about my job, and I told them I'd rather not. See, frankly, Cannon Mills had become a way of life for me. See, I'm an old lady now. I really wasn't afraid of getting fired but I'd rather they talked to some of the young ones. I told them that some of the others could take the lead this time and I would be there to support them. Right then I couldn't tell why I didn't want to. Well, oh, my neighbors came down here and they just blessed me out for not taking the lead in this suit. See, I had been the first woman hired at Cannon Mills and I had been a leader politically in the community. I said, "I'm not ready for it." I was really thinking more about my daughter's scholarship and my other daughter's work. This suit was all everywhere, in the *New York Times*, on national news. But the ones that did sue got a lot of money in back wages.

But you know, you'd be surprised. Me and Mary Lee are very outgoing and we worked there more than a year before they hired any other black women on the first shift and I can call up those white women I worked with or they call me up and we just talk.

See, your work, and this goes for white people and black, is what you are. You associate with the same kind of people on the weekends that you work with during the week. Your work is your life. There is a lot of courtship and lovemaking going on right there in the mill. There's a lot of stuff both good and bad going on right there in the mill. The mill is a way of life. When we black women came in there, this was just a new area of life that was opened up to those white women as well as for us. When we first went to work in the mill, they had a toilet built on the outside just for us. They told us we could go anywhere in the mill we wanted to but that was the one that was for us. Now why would they build a new little outhouse out there if it wasn't because they didn't know how it was going to work. It was a little house out there and on one side was "Colored Men" and the other side "Colored Women." And the water fountain said "Colored." That lasted about a year. But people were extremely nice, I mean, they looked at us like they just wondered, "Well what they going to do?"

Even now you know some of them are so afraid of us. Not afraid that we going to do something to them, but, you know, I think the majority of the black people in the mill are just a little more intelligent than the white people. I mean things that I took for granted they didn't know about. Like politics. "I don't never vote," they'd say. "I don't never vote." And I keep up with that stuff, I got to know, I been voting since I was twenty-one. I remember the day that Kennedy was assassinated, we had been

Corine Lytle Cannon, 1984.
Photo by the author.

talking about political things all that day and at break time I would just get on my little soap box and do my thing. I've had as many as twenty people stand around listening to what I said. We'd be talking about whatever was happening like redistricting. We had to vote about redistricting one time. And I'd tell them to go vote. "Well, they gonna do what they gonna do anyway," they'd say. And I remember when Goldwater was running and I'd try to tell them that if it's gonna be hard for black people, you white people gonna suffer too. And this one white man, he was such a Republican, and he'd talk back to me and we'd get into it at dinner time. And I'd done read up on what was happening and I'd tell him, "The only difference between you and me is that you're white." And I'd say, "Any day in the week if God wanted to make me over and make me white I wouldn't want to be. I don't want to be nothing but what I am and I definitely don't want to be white." And I'd tell him that. And I'd go on talking like that and they'd say, "She's right, y'all better go on and register to vote." But there was a lot of things that they didn't know about.

As far as the racial tension, now this is the truth, the blacks would mention it a whole lot more than the whites. I mean, like if somebody told me to do something I didn't want to do, I'd say, "Just because I'm black, you think I'm gonna do that? I got news for you, you better remember them good old days because they're gone forever." I'd say that to my boss man or anybody and usually they'd turn all kinds of red. Or they'd say, "I'm looking for those colored boys," and I'd say, "Looking for what? I didn't know they hired little boys in here, everything I saw in here is mens." And see, then white people would learn that you didn't use the words "colored boys," that you said "black men." They'd say, "Did any of you see those colored boys that supposed to be around here?" And we'd all say, "Where'd ya see 'em? Tell 'em to come back here, ain't no little boys supposed to be in here." Then he'd say, "Oh, I mean them black men."

I felt like we was educating them sometimes. Particularly the day Martin Luther King got killed. I said on the way to work, "Oh God, please don't let me get upset today, let me keep my cool." We got there and people were really upset. Everybody was upset because we didn't know what was happening. And the word came that they were burning down Washington and four or five buses of our children were in Washington. They'd gone on their high school trip. So they were up there and we were worried sick. My daughter called home. They had been to the Smithsonian and they saw these black people marching by, and they saw my daughter with her school class, and they were asking why she was with these white people and they made more slurs to her than to the whites. So I gave them the number of some cousins I had up there and they all went down in the basement of these cousins and just cried.

So that day I said I wasn't going to get all upset and I went on in to work. I walked into the mill and these girls were crying and one of them said, "This is the first time I ever shed a tear over a colored person." And I just blessed her out. I just blessed her out. I said, "Now, have you ever heard anything so stupid. People are people." I said, "Christ died for everybody. Martin Luther King was killed. Why you have to feel guilty because you want to cry? Cry if you want to. Why you have to feel guilty for crying for him? You're just so stupid. So stupid. If you want to cry, cry. You don't see me crying. I feel like it's a victory. Martin Luther King said he'd been to the mountain top and he didn't have nothing to worry about. He said in his speech, 'I'd like to live a long time,' but he knew that any day not worth dying for ain't worth living for." And then everybody got quiet. And I shouted out, "If you want to cry, cry." I said, "Stupid thing, over here crying over Martin Luther King and feeling guilty because he was black." Then I went on over to my section and this white man said, "Well he knew something was going to happen the way he was disrupting everything," and I just turned around and blessed him out. I said, "He had a purpose. He had a purpose. And that was his purpose." I said, "When you've served the purpose that God put you here for, then you go on away. You don't live not one minute after your purpose." So he shut up. So then they'd come over there and tell me, "They talking, you better go shut them up." And I'd say, "Here, watch my job 'til I get back." That day, I was ready for 'em.

You know, if things had been different, if the establishment had been different, I would be doing something different. I don't know that I would be any happier, but I would be doing something different. Now, I'm not a degreed person, but the best thing that has ever happened to black women in the South in my lifetime is a chance to be full-fledged citizens. And that comes from their work. You can't even pretend to be free without money. Now, I've been all over this area and the majority of black women in the South are very intelligent. If a black woman could get into the federal government, which I know is impossible now, but if a group of black women could get in there, they would clean up this deficit that Reagan has built up. It would be different, but we wouldn't have that deficit. How wasteful people are. The majority of white people can't understand how black people make it. I can't remember when I didn't have a dollar. I had six children in school at all times. And they all went to college. And I had 'em all in kindergarten. I never missed a school trip. I never got any assistance. We could straighten this country out, all this waste that's going on, because we've been taught that you can make do, that where there's a will there's a way, and how to make a way out of no way.

SHIFTING FOR CHANGE

The textile industry seeks out new labor markets from among the world's poorest peoples and recruits a largely female workforce. It is an industry that has a history of fighting organized labor before leaving an area for another primarily agrarian and industrially backward region.

Probably because spinning, weaving, and the fashioning of textiles have traditionally been thought of as women's work, the industry has been successful in engaging women worldwide in their first opportunity to work at wage labor, thus giving them a chance to live more independent lives. With their own money, women are not as dependent on their families for economic support, and with this new independence comes the promise of decision-making power. Once a part of the mill metropolis, however, southern mill women found themselves living under the power of the mill owner, who seemed to be present in nearly every facet of their lives. In the churches, for example, if a preacher did not preach a sermon that supported hard work here on earth with just rewards awaiting in heaven, it was not unusual for that preacher to be removed by the mill owners who financially supported nearly every institution in town.

It is this pervasive domination with which southern mill women have had to deal when organizing themselves for better wages, better working conditions, and compensation for the deadly disease of brown lung. Historically, when a southern mill woman decided to join an organizing drive, she risked losing not only her job in the mill—which might be the only industry in town that hired women—but her only means of subsistence, her house, her credit, and in some cases, her life. Southern mill woman and union activist Ella Mae Wiggins was shot dead with a bullet in the head during the Gastonia strike in 1929, as was mill woman and organizer Sandi Smith in 1979 during a demonstration against the Ku Klux Klan.

Mill women continue to come up against oppression on a daily basis. Southern mill women's strength lies not so much in their ability to organize successfully to counter the tactics of the powerful textile industry, but in their ability to survive poverty, humiliation, and isolation from the rest of the world. There is no room for weakness in this life. One learns to carefully weigh risk and to fight only those battles where there is a chance of winning. Given such odds, those mill women who have dared to speak out—and there have been many—are to be recognized, clearly, as conscious and courageous women.

GLADYS GRIFFIN

Greensboro, North Carolina

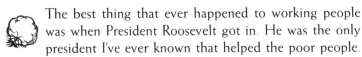The best thing that ever happened to working people was when President Roosevelt got in. He was the only president I've ever known that helped the poor people. You don't know nothing about the Depression when Hoover was in but I do. You couldn't buy a job hardly. Roosevelt raised the legal age for work and got those younguns out of the mill. He made jobs. He put people to work digging ditches, anything he could find to make a job for a person, that's what he done. He cut our hours down from twelve hours a day to eight hours a day, and the mill owners couldn't cut our pay. We wasn't making much to start with, and the pay in the mill didn't go up from then to amount to anything until we got the union and they had to raise the pay.

The worst thing that ever happened to mill workers is letting the boss man run over them and being scared of their jobs. Now I would think that was about the two worst things I know of. I've seen a lot of that, oh yeah, and the people was afraid to talk back to their boss man because they was afraid that they'd get fired. I ain't somebody that likes for somebody to tell me to do something. If you was to tell me I *had* to do something I'd see you dead in hell before I done it. But now if you asked me to do something in a nice way, if I wanted to do it, I'd say all right. But if I told you no, you needn't ask me no more because I ain't gonna do it.

My mother was pretty much like me. She was very frankly spoken and when she told you to do something you better do it.

She was serious about her work on her job. She was a weaver. I believe she went to work in the cotton mill when my oldest sister was a baby. She was in her twenties. She was born in 1886, so that was probably around 1910. I don't even know how old she was when she got married, I just remember it was before you had to have a marriage license. My mother and me didn't have time to do much together 'cause she was always working and back then that was twelve hours a day. When she was home, she was cooking and preparing clothes for us to wear and, apart from the housework that was done on the weekend, she done that. Of course all us children had our chores to do, those that were old enough and big enough to do anything. I've been cooking and washing dishes ever since I could stand up in a chair. My father was never there for us, just in and out. My stepfather walked off and left my mother when we was living in Haw River in the winter of 1925. So you could just say my mother was a single parent.

We lived in a little old house with crazy younguns running everywhere. The most we ever had to play with was to play sticks, jump rope, hopscotch, hide-n-seek, jack rocks, and things like that. Didn't have much of anything. I remember one time I took my sister Myrtle and went to the woods and made her a dress out of leaves. Took straw and made pins out of it and made her a dress out of leaves. Just playing. We didn't have nothing to play with like children do now.

Everywhere we ever lived was a mill village and they was all about the same. We had a hard time but we always had plenty to eat, such as it was, we had plenty to eat. If I ever went hungry a day in my life, it was because I was too lazy to go fix something to eat. I've known my mother a many times to get up on Sunday morning and say, "Well, I don't know what we going to have for dinner, there ain't a thing in the house to cook." But when we went to dinner, we had as good a meal as ever there was put on the table.

We had a rough time coming up, we didn't have things like other families where there was three or four in the family. They was nine of us younguns and when one of us got old enough, we had to go to work to help support the family. And we'd give our mother our money because that was what we were supposed to do. I went to work in the mill when I was ten. I went in as a spinner at the Sugarhill Cotton Mill in Haw River, North Carolina in 1924. We helped support the family this way. Mother would buy what we wore and everything, and she provided good for us. We didn't have fancy things, I don't think we had but one feather bed and that was in her room. The rest of us slept on straw beds. We didn't even know what a mattress was. We'd live in anywhere from three- to five-room houses, most of them were four rooms. The boys slept in one bedroom and the girls and mother slept in the others, two and three to a bed. We never had a living room, never knowed what a linoleum or carpet was until after we was all grown. We cooked on a wood stove and had a wood heater or a fireplace. You'd stand at the fireplace and your legs would burn and your bottom would be freezing. Mother bought our first radio a little before the Lindbergh baby died, because I remember hearing about the Lindbergh child on the radio, but we didn't have time to listen to it much.

We always had work to do in the mill or at home, in the garden, and everywhere we lived Mother always had pigs to raise. We'd raise our own meat if we had a place where we could have a hog lot. We'd have chickens for eggs, we'd have a garden out in the back yard, and we'd can stuff. There wasn't a blade of grass in the yard except in the garden. We'd have somebody come and break the ground and then we'd use hoes to work the garden. One time an old man's mule fell dead plowing up our garden and we like to never got that thing moved.

We lived on the mill hill and then we moved kinda outta the city down near the railroad. The first night we was there that train came through at two o'clock in the morning and we hadn't got all our dishes unpacked but what was sitting there on the table. When that train come by, oh what a noise, and everything in the house rattled, the dishes rattled, the window lights rattled. Finally Mother said, "Well, if you'll just wait I'll get up and open the door and let you come on through the house." That's how close we was to the railroad tracks. We got our first oil stove when we lived there.

We moved so much because I don't know, Mother just wasn't never satisfied with her job. She always wanted to just be a weaver. They put her in the spinning room to start with, then she worked in the spool room for a while, but she didn't like that so she quit. She wanted to work where they was making that pretty cloth. She didn't even know the name of it or what kind of job it was. I don't remember where she finally went to weaving at.

She put all her younguns in the mill. Me and Myrtle and Cicero went to the spinning room, J.C. and Frances went to the hosiery mill, and the rest 'cept one was sent to Burlington Mills. Raymond had infantile paralysis and for a long time he couldn't get a job. Finally he got a job at Burlington cleaning up offices and such as that. He does what they tell him to do in the sample room. If it's mop the room he'll go get the mop and do it. Yeah, she put all her younguns in the mill.

I reckon Mother would get unhappy with her job or mad at her boss man and just quit. Back then, before 1930, you wouldn't have no trouble finding a job, you could get a job anywhere. If she didn't like a place, she'd be through and get a job somewhere else. This was when I was a child and it was that way up until we moved to Gibsonville in the late 1920s and that's where we got stuck. None of the other kids liked it when we moved there, but it was all right with me, I didn't care. I always made friends everywhere we moved. Used to have a lot of fights though. I'd fight about anything. I reckon I was the only one in the whole bunch that would fight like that, and I reckon I got tanned more than any of the rest of them did too.

Me and Myrtle went to work when I was ten and she was eleven. We couldn't go to school because we had to go to work. We had to go to work to help Mother buy groceries and things. It was that way for us children all the way from the oldest to the youngest. The younger they got, the more of a chance to go to school they was. I lied about my age and Myrtle did too to go to work in the mill. When we moved to Thomasville and I went to work in the cotton mill there, they laid me off the first shift, so I lied again and told them I was eighteen so I could go to work on the overnight shift and I still wasn't but about fifteen then. I lied so much about my age I like to never have got my age straightened out. Of course it was down right in the family Bible, but they run it up so we could go to work in the mill. A kid used to be able to go to work in the mill at nine years old. Boys and girls, so long as they was big enough to reach the spinning frame or whatever they had for them to do, they went to work. It wasn't just in my family, it was all cotton mill people. Children back then didn't have a chance to go to school. You couldn't start until you was seven and I stayed sick with colds and pneumonia so much that I didn't have a chance to go to school. Parents didn't believe in school like they do now, so when those older kids got old enough they went to work in the mill.

I don't remember nothing of my first day at work other'n being scared to death, scared of the machinery 'cause I'd never seen none. I didn't know what I was going to learn to do, but it didn't take that woman but a few minutes to show me. She had me putting up ends in one day. Now they give them six weeks to learn. I worked in the cotton mill for forty-seven years, from 1924 to 1971. Now you can't even get a job, but back before the Depression they was begging for people to work. Cone Mills had a rule that if you lived in a cotton mill house and your children didn't go to work in the mill, you got throwed off the mill hill. You had to go somewhere else to live even if you worked in the mill. If you wouldn't put your younguns in that cotton mill, you wouldn't have a place to live. You had to go find yourself some place to live. So I grew up in a cotton mill.

By the time I was grown, the women I worked with, some of them was nice and some of them wasn't. I'd say the majority of them was pretty nice people. We didn't do nothing except work together 'cause we didn't have time, we was all raising our young-uns. Just work and raise your younguns was all we had time to do. I left home when my daughter was eight years old and went to live in a boarding house. I moved out of Mother's to be on my own. We had a lot of fun there at the boarding house, sat around playing cards, sat around and talked. People would just come and go. Then I got me an apartment on Seaver Street in Greensboro. My sister at home took care of my baby for me while I was working. It was pretty rough trying to make it all on my salary. I was making $13.50 a week when I went to White Oak to work in 1937. I bought groceries, paid my trolley fares to and from work, sent four dollars home a week for my daughter's keeping, and bought coal for my coal stove and oil for my oil heater. Then I paid rent on my one-room apartment. That all came to about $13.50 a week.

Mother was still working in the mill at the time too. She worked in the mill until she was in her seventies. Then she would have gone on working had she not got mad at her boss man. He had told her she had to do something and she looked straight at him and told him, "Let me tell you one thing, I don't have to work in this cotton mill. I'm seventy-two years old, I can retire." Then she stopped off her job and went home. And she never went back. They tried to get her to come back but she wouldn't do it. I knew that was the only way she'd quit, if they made her mad.

You better believe I've got mad too, but like Mother I always quit before I got fired. I never was threatened to be fired but one time. I did my job at the cotton mill better than I did my job at home, because I was getting paid in the mill and at home I wasn't making any money. I had a boss man one time say that he could tell a clean housekeeper because of the way they did their job in the mill. I was standing right there and I said, "You're a liar." He said, "As clean as you keep your work you bound to be a good housekeeper." I said, "I get paid for what I do here; as far as home, it can go, I don't care. I don't get paid to work there." Oh I had plenty of arguments with the boss man but I never did get fired. I had one who accused me of punching a hole in a bedspread. I was supposed to inspect these bedspreads and if I found a kinky filling in it, I was supposed to cut it and tie it off, but some of them holes was so big you couldn't tie them off. So he went and told a lie on me and said I punched a hole in a bedspread and I told him I didn't do it. He said, "You're a damn liar, you did do it too." I said, "You're another damn liar, I didn't do it. I cut it off and tied if off like you told me to." So he reported me for calling him a damn liar. Well that made me mad. I said, "Yes, I cussed him back the same way he cussed me." So they left me alone.

It was while I was working at White Oak that I helped get the union down there. It was after Roosevelt was in because they had cut the work day down to eight hours a day. The first time they tried to get a union in, they put machine guns on top of the buildings and the National Guard was called out because they didn't want no union in there. Just didn't want them to have a union 'cause, see, it would have made the cotton mill people more independent, they could demand more things of the mill owners. If we got a union they had to run things according to seniority, and if you had a problem you could take it to the shop steward and they would take it to the overseer.

Somebody came up to me one day and started talking union when they was stretching us out. Oh it was a deep dark secret at first. I joined it and in the beginning there weren't but a very few. I asked a lot of people to join and I told them we'd need the union if we was going to have any rights at all. When we got the union organized they was a lot of people who joined it and wouldn't go through with it. When I first went to work in there we was running seven and eight sides. Then, when they first stretched us out, they gave us ten. I was spinning when we first called a strike. By then they was going to give us twenty sides. So we went on strike. At that time, we didn't have no contract so nobody was paying dues. See, the union didn't keep you up then. We didn't have no money and everybody had to go in debt. Didn't pay rent or nothing.

We had quite a few that was out on strike for maybe three or four weeks. We stopped the freight trains from going in and most of the trucks. If the trucker was a union man, he wouldn't cross the picket line. The railroad company never crosses a picket line. They had to call a white-collar man in from Salisbury to ship out

A mill strike in
the 1950s.
*Photo courtesy of
the Library of
Congress.*

the stock. That's when the owners of this mill, the Cones, started buying their own trucks. We never had but one man fail to stop that belonged to a union. He said that he had a government order to go in and ship that stock out and he showed it to us. See, this was during World War II and they needed our stock for uniforms. And you better believe I walked on the picket line—that was a lot of fun and a lot of hard work. I carried a sign that had our union number on it and talked to people and got them to sign up. I was shop steward and later I was president of the union down there. A lot of the workers didn't want to go on strike because they was afraid of their jobs, afraid they'd get fired, but we went down there and stood in the middle of the tracks and stopped the train. Sat down on the side of the tracks and talked to the engineers. They just came on out and sat there on the grass and talked to us.

We was striking for better wages and better working conditions. We got our contract and got a raise in pay, but the working conditions kept getting worse. They kept changing the machinery and the more they done the more they added on you. If somebody was out sick, some of the spinners running ten sides would take twelve, some would take fourteen, and I'd say, "You're asking for more work." I never doubled up a day in my life. I wouldn't double up for them. I said I would do my job and nobody else's. And when they tried to get me to learn people to spin, I said, "I ain't never learnt myself." I said, "If you want somebody to learn to spin, you'll have to put them with somebody besides me." Because it was double work on you, they paid you a little extra to learn them but it wasn't enough. I told them I had all I could do. They would go ask the hands if they would run extra sides for them and said that they could make a little extra money that way, but eventually it became required that we all had to run that many. Pretty soon we was running twenty sides for what we was running ten for. That's when we struck.

BESSIE HENSLEY

High Point, North Carolina

I remember that day. I didn't walk off my job, I just went to the mill gate and when they said they was going to strike I just didn't go no further. Everybody did. We had what we called a commissary and we'd give out food. I worked in the commissary every week that it was open. You know, they'd have three-member, four-member families and so on, and we'd have so much we'd put in a box for each family. Most of it was canned stuff, dried beans, potatoes, and stuff like that. On the picket line we'd just laugh and have a big time. It was cold but we did it. That lasted down there a long time. We'd cook and eat down there in a tent. We'd take dried beans and stuff like that down there and cook 'em. Either that or cook 'em at home and take it down there. Everybody would get together and eat. Then we'd feed the kids when they come home from school. I felt like we did a good job of surviving. Then some of 'em that was running the strike went back to work. I told 'em that they went coward and left us in the wide open and then we had nothin'. I remember some of the women went in to work one day and some of the women on the picket line jumped on 'em and beat the hell out of 'em. Well, I didn't care one bit 'cause they had no business crossing that picket line. If those cowards had stayed out of there, we'd have got our contract. Then it would have been a good place to work and we could have made a better living.

I never been above my raising. My daddy took an old mule we had and scooped out the reservoir for the Amazon Cotton

Mill in Thomasville. He was a young man then, 'fore I was ever born. I'm not shamed of my raising. I'm proud. I was raised poor, but I was raised clean and honest. They was twelve children in my family and ten of them lived to become adults. We all lived in a three-room house. The room I was born in had a fireplace, a good-sized fireplace, big enough to keep us warm. In the kitchen was a long table and a wood stove. Mama and Daddy and the baby slept in the front room and we kids slept in the back bedroom. Daddy was a farmer. He raised tobacco, wheat, corn, and one year I 'member him a havin' cotton. He rented his farming land, and we kids worked on the farm. Did anything that needed to be done. We worked in the fields every day until the crop was gathered, but we seldom worked in the fields after twelve o'clock on Saturday. We come up with the cows at twelve unless there was something we had to get done. That's the reason none of us ever got no education, we had to stay at work.

We wanted to go to work in the cotton mill to get out of the fields. All us kids worked in the mill 'cept the younger ones who worked at home. Then as they got older they would go to work in the mill. Some of 'em went to work in the mill as young as nine years old. Back then they could go to work in the mill that young, but I was between fifteen and sixteen. By then they had passed a law that you couldn't go to work so young. I went to work at the Amazon Cotton Mill and worked a couple of weeks and then they found out I wasn't sixteen. So Clyde, my brother, was working at the Jewell Cotton Mill and he got me a job up there. I went to work there sometime in the spring and I was almost sixteen. I worked on the third shift. They learnt me to spool and they didn't pay me until I had learnt where I could do it. Then they commenced to paying me. I worked there until times got bad and they laid a bunch of us off. Then I went to High Point to the Highland Mill and stayed with a lady over there. She kept boarders.

Then went up and stayed with another lady and kept her kids. She was 'specting a baby. When she quit to have her baby, at the Highland they let me have her job. That's the way I went to work at the Highland. Her husband and Earl worked in the mill together down there at the Highland. He come up there on Saturday, Earl did, and they was going off. I was sweeping the porch. When this man went out to get in the car with Earl, his wife told me to tell him not to stay out so late because I was going home. So I told him, and Earl he started mouthing back at me. I don't 'member now what he did say, but I told him that if he didn't get out of there I'd hit him with that broom. So that's how I met my husband and it went on for a long time. I was nineteen in December and I married in February. Daddy didn't care but Mama didn't like it. She didn't care for me a-going with Earl, but she didn't want me to marry. She wanted to keep me and all the rest. All of us I reckon slipped off and got married 'cept the youngest ones. Mama needed the money we older ones was a-bringing in from the mill. We gave our money to her, all of us did. She'd go out and buy groceries with it, and if we got anything to wear she bought it. She needed our little old checks to live on. You see, they didn't have incomes like they do now. They didn't have no social security or welfare or food stamps then.

After I got married, the first mill house we lived in was a little three-room house that set there next to the mill. Right beside the mill. They've torn it away now. You could see the mill from the bedroom window, the kitchen window, the front room window, from anywhere you wanted to, you could just look out, the mill was always there. It was just a plain wooden house, an old house. We heated with a heater, a coal heater, and a wood stove in the kitchen. But it was a house, you know; back then during the Depression if you had a house at all you was lucky. Then they had what they called a wildcat strike while we was livin' in this little house. I wasn't workin', it was just 'fore Jack was born, but Earl was workin' then. There was a bunch of mill people who come down there and just picked the fence up and tore it up because they wouldn't unlock the gate. Then they went in and they went marching down through the mill wanting people to get out of there. I was out but Earl was there.

Bessie Hensley with her son, about 1935.
Photo courtesy of Bessie Hensley.

You see, they didn't have no union there then. But then later years they had a big strike and we all walked out. I don't 'member what year it was, but it was after World War II, 'cause Earl and me both was a-workin' in the mill then. We joined the union. We sure did. Went to meetings and paid our dues. They had got the union during the war, but after the war was over they told the hands the gold rush was over and they never would sign another contract. Well, we went on strike and stayed out for months and months. I 'member that day, I didn't walk off my job. I just went to the mill gate and when they said they was a goin' to strike I just didn't go no further. Everybody did. They wasn't but one or two that went in that day. Then after that didn't nobody go in. I 'spect we stayed on strike for a year or more.

The reason we went on strike was to keep the mill from treating the hands just any old way. Like, now in the mill you just have to get your dinner when you can. On the farm you could stop and go to the house and eat, but in the mill you work straight through eight hours and if you get caught up you eat. Sometimes you get to eat and sometimes you don't. Oh God, you mean stop off the machines and let us eat? They'd have a heart attack! Now they used to do that when I first went to work, they'd stop. But boy, they got to where they just worked straight through and sometimes you got to go and sometimes you wouldn't. You'd have just long enough to eat what you had, sometimes five minutes, sometimes ten, and then sometimes you'd just take a bite and go. I've eaten while I worked. Laid my food in the trough with the bobbins.

If you had to go to the bathroom you just had to leave your work and get behind. The machines kept going. A lot of girls who worked with me had problems on account of not being able to go to the bathroom. And the mill, inside was like a fog of cotton, you know, dust. It would make your nose itch and you couldn't half breathe. Earl, he can't hardly get his breath, they is something wrong with his lungs. But I worked in it, you just learn to do a lot of things. And I didn't pay much attention to the noise then, but now my hearing on one side is pretty bad.

Then, I know when Mama died, I was out and they was supposed to pay vacation pay. I was out a week and they knew Mama had died, but when it come time for us to get our vacation pay in September, I didn't get none. I asked about it and the strawboss told me it was because I was out and didn't report in.

Since I fell and hurt my back, I haven't worked any. Yep. You know, they had shellac floors over in the White Oak Mill where I worked. Somebody had spilt some water or Coke on the floor and I slipped on it. Just set my whole weight down and there was somethin' that popped in my back and plumb up my spine. Yep. They have first aid for people in the mill who get hurt, but what made me so mad about when I fell was that they carried me to the first-aid room and they stood there for a long time arguing whether they was goin' to take me to the hospital or not. The nurse finally said that she felt like I ought to go on, so I told her to call Earl, my husband—he was home cooking supper. She said she had to ask the overseer if she could 'cause we lived in the next town and it was a toll call. I said, "Call him collect, he'll accept it. Tell him to come over here, I'm goin' to the hospital." Finally she called him. I fell around three o'clock, and it was six o'clock 'fore they put me to bed in the hospital. After that I couldn't work no more. I got workmen's compensation out of that, but I had to get a lawyer and fight for it. We had to go to court. It took 'em a year or two to settle it because the company didn't want to pay off. I reckon they just thought I was puttin' on. And I still ain't able to do nothin' that I have to lift or anything like that. They offered me different jobs in the mill but they wasn't a thing I could do. If they had been I would have been there yet.

I was working seven days a week when I got hurt, but when they first started to pay me workmen's compensation they just averaged me for what I was makin' for forty hours. I got to countin' it up one day and I told Earl that that wasn't right. So I went over there and told my lawyer about it. They had a trial over it and the judge told 'em that Cone Mills had a record of every day and every dollar I had made, so if they owed me money I'd get it, and I did. But, you know, every time I went to the doctor they'd call and want me to go back to work. See, if they could have got me back in the mill, you understand, I wouldn't have got any disability. No, I told the doctor when I went there, I wasn't able to work. And he said, "Well, they wantin' you to come back and I don't see nothin' wrong with you." So I went and got me another doctor and he found my problem. Then I went and got me a lawyer and we went to court. If them at the mill had taken me to the hospital when I first got hurt and if the doctor had put me in either a cast or a brace, then I believe my back would finally have got to where I could have went back to work. But you see, he didn't put me in the bed, and I sit drawn up all the time. I couldn't lay down. The first day they got me up, I was drawn up plumb over to where I had to hold onto the nurse to take me to the bathroom. That doctor didn't treat me like no doctor. He treated me just like what he was—a company man.

Mill work is hard work. Those days were hard days and we just had to take it. If we refused, we just wouldn't have had no jobs. There was a lot of people who lost their job because they wouldn't do what they was told. This is why a union is a good thing, see, if it's carried out. If they was good people that owned the plant and would work with the people, they wouldn't need no union. Now you take a plant, sometimes the boss man thinks he's better than the help. But it's like this. If the help wasn't there the boss man wouldn't have a job, and if the boss man wasn't there, the overseers and the people who owned the mill wouldn't have nothing. That's the way I look at public work. It takes the floor sweeper on up to keep a plant runnin'.

NOLA STALEY

Greensboro, North Carolina

 My first job in the mill was terrible. I started out doffing because the boys was all in the army, you know, and doffing was a boy's job. I didn't like it, it was too hard. We had so many frames to doff and when we went around and doffed them all one time, then we got a break, if we were fast enough. They run every four hours. And when we went around the second time and got through maybe twenty or thirty minutes before quitting time, then we could go home. It was terrible but I was just glad I had a job, because jobs was hard to come by. You couldn't hardly find a job before World War II started. When I was sixteen, you couldn't buy a job in Montgomery County. I mean they wasn't no jobs. World War II came along and they was more jobs and less people to do them. In July of '43 I went to winding. The winding machines had timers on them that wound, say, eighteen to twenty-three bobbins a minute. I didn't think my job was dangerous, though now I have cut myself and had to go to the emergency room several times, but never nothing serious.

But don't even bother asking what the air was like in the mill because you don't want me to get all riled up in telling you. It got better as the years went by, I'll put it that way, but it was bad to start off with, especially in the winding room. Revolution Mill was pretty clean. I mean, it wasn't clean, it was a little better. But I've stood and wound, and you have to stand in one place for that, and the lint would be up over my ankles. But what is bad is when the sweeper comes and sweeps around you and leaves that big old pile there in the floor of nothing in the world but ground up cotton burrs. That's what it is. And that fan is blowing, going around and around over your head, you know, it blows that stuff all over you. At quitting time you comb through your hair and you get a handful of cotton out. Any time you are out of work for two or three days and go back to work it will just eat you to death. You get your nose raw rubbing it. It irritates you a while, but you get used to it.

These last few years, since 1975 I guess, they have these masks you can wear. But anybody who's got a breathing problem in the first place can't breathe through that thing. Oh Lord, I've tried to wear them. I could wear them long enough to blow my machine off or for somebody else to blow it off, and that's about as long as I could wear them. I've reached up and just tore them off my face trying so hard to get my breath. I just could not wear them.

The air is the worst when they clean in your department and they're blowing with them air hoses to clean the machines. They have to clean the machines or after a while they would get knee-deep in cotton. They blow it off the machines and sweep it up. Like at White Oak, for instance, they was twelve machines in the winding room when I worked there and they was twelve winders. They was room just enough for somebody else to walk between the machines. I've stood and worked this winder with them a-cleaning that winder beside me, and they would blow all in that machine and that stinking greasy cotton would blow all in my face and make my nose and throat burn. Now that operator would be stopped off and sent somewhere else while they cleaned her machine, which they usually cleaned them about every two weeks. They went around cleaning one a day. I've stood and run this one while they cleaned that one and they blowed that stuff all over me. Then when I started having breathing problems and the doctors started telling me something was wrong, I started stopping off my machine. And I'd sit down while they cleaned the one beside me. I wouldn't stand there and run one while they cleaned the other'n. But by then I'd eaten that stuff for twenty or twenty-five years and it was too late. The bosses didn't like it when I stopped my machine off, but they knew they couldn't do nothing about it because they knew I had a problem. I have stopped it off and told them I had to go see the nurse and go and sit down in first aid until I thought they was through cleaning up. Before then I would just stand there and run my machine through it all.

I didn't find out I had a breathing problem, they did. I knew there was something wrong with me but it never dawned on me what was wrong. I just knew that, well frankly, I thought I had heart trouble. I kept telling my doctor, "I hurt in my chest but I don't know why." He kept telling me I had arthritis. He had me taking medicine for arthritis. Then once a year over there at White Oak you had to take the breathing test. So in February of 1976, some lady come to the first aid room and sent for me to come to first aid. She asked me all kinds of questions and gave me a TB test and I don't know what all she asked me now. Then she sent me back to work. Two or three weeks later the doctor sent for me, Dr. Martin, and he asked me all kinds of questions, and I answered them. Well, he wanted me to quit. He said I needed to get out of there, that I'd live longer if I got out of that dust. I asked him if he was going to help me get on disability. He said, "No, I don't think you're sick enough to get on disability." I said, "Well, you say I'm too sick to work." He said that first they wanted to transfer me to the weave room on third shift, but I couldn't take my seniority to another department, and I didn't know one thing in the world about the weave room, so I wouldn't go. I said, "You don't want to do a dern thing but put blue lint on my white lint." See, in the weave room the warped yarn is dyed blue and the filling we make is white. It goes out of the weave room and is wove in that blue warp until a pair of jeans all look blue, but the filling in there is really white. Any lint in that weave room, and at that time the lint out there was pretty bad, was blue lint. I told Dr. Martin that he wasn't going to do a thing in the world except put blue lint on top of the white lint that I already had in my lungs. So I wouldn't go to the weave room. They held that against me in my compensation, because the mill said they offered to transfer me to a different department and I wouldn't transfer. But there wasn't no difference. The lint was the same out there as it was in the winding room, just blue.

Dr. Martin made me an appointment and sent me to a lung specialist that worked for the Cones. The Cones was paying for it and paid me for two days' work. I had to go one day and take all kinds of tests and they took x-rays and he told me to get out of that mill and quit smoking or I wouldn't live two years. This was about April or May of '76. I worked on to '78. I was fifty-eight years old when they told me I couldn't work in the mill no more.

I was a member of the Brown Lung Association even when I was working in the mill. My best friend down there at the mill was a member and she got me to join. At one time her husband was president of it. Naomi, his wife, and I used to eat together. I filed for compensation when they finally told me I couldn't work there no more. We had a hearing and I was awarded twelve thousand dollars. Well, nine thousand dollars. Three thousand dollars went for lawyer fees.

Back about a year and a half ago, they offered me twelve thousand dollars and my doctor's bills for as long as I lived, and my lawyer appealed it. Then months later, maybe nine or ten months later, my lawyer decided we shouldn't appeal, we should take the twelve thousand dollars. After he knew the Morrison case was lost, he decided we shouldn't appeal. He told me if I would take up my appeal I could get my money in thirty days. So I said, "Well, you're the lawyer. Do what you think."

In the Morrison case, this mill woman was asking for total disability. She had brown lung and she smoked. Everybody to their own opinion and I don't care who knows it, I said it right up there in the Brown Lung Office in front of them all, I don't think they ought to pay her total disability. I don't think anybody who smokes cigarettes should get total disability. Cigarettes hurt you. But so does cotton dust. I know I've been a lot better since I came out of that mill. I never smoked more than a pack of cigarettes a day. I don't want any more than what is due me. But twelve thousand dollars, that's nothing! Cone Mills didn't want to give that to me. Oh no! I had to fight for it. The Industrial Commission awarded me that money. Then the contract said that they would pay my doctor bills for as long as I live, but they sure ain't paid none. I had eleven hundred dollars worth of doctor's bills when I finally got my check for twelve thousand dollars, which took me three years. I turned in eleven hundred dollars worth of receipts and I haven't heard a thing from it. So I don't know if they are going to pay it or not. They were supposed to. My hearing was in '78 and I got my money in '81. Well, the day I got that money, I came home and went down to Federal Savings and took one thousand dollars out of the bank and bought a six-month certificate because neither one of us has a speck of hospital insurance in the world. I guess I will have Medicare but my husband has nothing. One of the main reasons I stayed in that mill was to have insurance. You never know when you going to have a big hospital bill, so I couldn't think of anything I needed more than to know that if I have to go into the hospital I have something to pay for it with.

I didn't exactly make out like a bandit on this deal. I don't know of anybody who was awarded as little as I was. I think the Industrial Commission is crooked. I think I got so little because I worked so much at the Brown Lung Office. I think that has something to do with it. I was on television a lot running my mouth. I lobbied in Raleigh. I was on Channel 2, "The Lee Kinnard Show." I was secretary of the Brown Lung Association one year. Last year we had this panel that was working on trying to hurry up cases and I was a part of that. You name it and we did it.

I'm supposed to take Dyalex. Some people take other things for brown lung. I'm supposed to take five tablets at seven a.m., at eleven a.m., at three p.m., at seven p.m. and at bedtime. That's five tablets each time, twenty-five tablets a day. When I first started going to Dr. Heathy, I couldn't walk as far as from the kitchen to the back door. I couldn't do anything. I couldn't even sweep the floor. I'm much better now. I don't take as many tablets

A demonstration by the Brown Lung Association.
Photo by Earl Dotter.

as I'm supposed to because see five hundred of them pills cost thirty-five dollars. If I took them like the prescription said to they wouldn't last me a month. I can't afford that. Some days are worse than others and on them I take more. Some days I don't take them but twice.

This aspirator helps me to breathe. This is something new that just came out and there was a big write-up in the paper about it. I took Loplin for a while but a bottle of those, which holds one thousand, is $110. These others here are what I first took when I started going to Dr. Heathy. You take thirty-five of these a day. My cough syrup costs fifteen dollars a bottle, but Robitussin helps a whole lot and is a lot cheaper. I didn't buy but a couple of those bottles of cough syrup before I went back to taking Robitussin. I couldn't afford it. If I took the medicine like I should it would run too high each month.

Let me get just a little bit of a cold and oh, I get sicker than anything. During an attack, when I start off with it, I feel like something is just smothering me, like pressing in on me, like a big piece of elastic drawing me in. Then I get shortwinded, so short of breath. But as I said, I'm better than I was. With me, I can get up in the morning and say, "Oh Lord, I'm getting a bad cold sure as the world. I'm going to be sick." It scares me to death to think I'm getting a bad cold. I just have to go to bed and just lay there. If I start coughing I'm done give out, feels like my heart is just going to stop beating. Then I'll go get four or five of the Dyaflex and these here lozenges and then I'll start getting better and I realize I don't have a cold. When I do actually get a cold I end up with about three trips to the doctor's for shots. I used to take penicillin but I don't take that no more. I take some kind of myacin. I had a real bad go-round last winter in February, but so far this winter I've been lucky. See, we take vitamins, all brown lung people take vitamins. I'm supposed to take ten vitamin C's, ten vitamin E's, and ten vitamin B6's every day. They run about $3.84 for a bottle of one hundred at K-Mart, something like that, for the C's and the B's. The E's are $5.84. So about fourteen dollars worth of vitamins would last me ten days if I took them like I should. I try to take four a day. If I took all my pills, that would be about sixty-five a day, but I don't believe my body could handle all that.

I used to have coughing spells, coughed 'til I spit blood, but since I got out of that dust I don't do that anymore. I used to get laryngitis every Monday. I'd be fine every Monday morning and about ten o'clock I'd be getting something like croup. By one o'clock break, I'm done hoarse, and I have many times not even been able to talk at one o'clock. I'd sound like a gourd. I'd come home by three and couldn't even do nothing but make grunting noises. I haven't had laryngitis since the last time I worked in that mill. By Tuesday, it wouldn't be so bad and Wednesday it would level out. Over the weekend when you were out of the mill, the stuff in your lungs would settle. So when you came back to work, it would get all stirred up again. That's what's called the Monday morning syndrome. My lawyer asked me one time how many days a week I worked, and I said, "Well, if I had worked seven days a week I'd a' been all right." I worked many a day sick, scared to lay out sick because I knew when I went in the next morning it would be another Monday morning. You didn't want to stay out on Wednesday because if you did, you knew Thursday was going to be another Monday morning.

Many a night I've slept right out there on that porch in a lounge chair 'cause I couldn't breathe in the bedroom. I wouldn't even think about going to bed without two big pillows. In other words, I had to sleep sitting up. In fact that was one of the things Dr. Martin was asking me when he called me into the first-aid room. He said, "And I bet you sleep on two big pillows." See he was trying to get me to quit, that's why he said it that way. A lot more mill workers have brown lung than they trying to make like. There have only been twelve mill workers from White Oak who have gotten compensation in the last three years, and about three from Revolution, but there's a whole lot more that's got claims in. Now Reagan is cutting back on the cotton dust standard because they say it has only affected one out of a hundred people. There are so many mill workers who never even knew they had it. All mill workers have relatives who coughed and carried on and died from it and never knew anything about brown lung.

My husband's father married this woman who lived over on White Oak hill. She slept in this little room that was built onto the house. She lived in one of the mill houses and had worked in the mill until she got to where she wasn't able. She had this little room built onto her house, like a little johnny house, just big enough for a bed. Where the window used to be in the house there was a door, and when you walked out there they wasn't a thing in there but a bed. She just had this little hull built onto the side of the house and all the way around it was windows. She sat and panted all the time. This was thirty years ago, and I wondered what was wrong with her then, but I never did know. She died a few years later and I never did know what was wrong with her. Sure as the world that woman had brown lung, but didn't nobody know nothing about it, not in this stupid country. Or so they say. England knew about it and has been paying compensation for years and years. In this country it wasn't even recognized as a disease until just a few years ago. And this is supposed to be such an advanced country.

Over at White Oak as soon as they give the workers a breathing test and find out they got brown lung, they going to try to get rid of them one way or the other. They going to tell you they'll transfer you to another department. Okay, so they do. You get in another department and you get so upset 'cause you can't learn your new job and you quit, or else they find another way of getting rid of you. I'm one of the ones it happened to! The Cones don't care about age, color, sex or what have you. They are for themselves. I never met one of the Cones. You don't think they going to come through there where we work with all that greasy cotton, do you?

White Oak was our model plant. All their people toured it. Revolution and Proximity didn't have tours. White Oak got all the tours. People from other countries and all the big shots went through White Oak. And you know why? Because if you wanted to tour the mill you had to go through the gate down there at the office. There's nowhere to get in except at the office, 'cause they got the gates all locked except at shift changing time. Okay, when you go in down there at the office, some smart person will call up the rest of the mill and say, "company's coming." And no matter what department you're in, somebody is going to stop and grab the brooms and start sweeping up the machines and sweeping the floors and polishing everything up, getting ready for company. Nobody ever went through without us knowing about it ahead of time. Oh yeah, you swept yourself to death. If the boss man got word at eight o'clock in the morning that somebody was coming and, if they didn't get there until two in the afternoon, you'd have swept until your legs give out. You couldn't stop, in case that company man came, that floor had to be clean. If they didn't know but three or four hours ahead of time, they'd stop off three or four hands to sweep.

I joined the union down at White Oak three or four times, but it was so sorry over there. Then you could almost get fired for paying your dues. Everybody acted like they was scared to death to have anything to do with the union. This was back in 1970 or '71. I know that the only working people in the United States that are making any money are working under a union. The ones that ain't union ain't making nothing. That's all I know. White Oak's got a union but it ain't a union. There's a difference. A few people pay dues over there, but what good is it? It ain't no good 'less the whole mill's union. You got to work together. It's got to be all or nothing to do any good. You take those people over there at the cigarette factory, they got good pay, good insurance, good retirement, 'cause they got a union. They got what Cone Mills ain't never had. Now in the last twenty years the mills that are unionized are helping the others out by setting the trend. In order to compete for the work force, the mills have to pay more. Still you don't make nothing. When I was there, though, the union had nothing to do with raises or cotton dust.

Somebody came to Revolution one time when I worked over there. Had her little tape recorder and sat in a little room out there next to first aid. Oh, it must have been around 1956. The boss man called certain people out there to talk to her. He said, "Go out there, this lady wants to talk to you." Okay, they sent me out there and I don't have no earthly idea what I told her, but she asked me, did I want my children to work in the mill? Well, she might as well have spit in my face. No, none of my children have ever worked in the mill. I don't want my children in that mill. I don't want my grandchildren in that mill. I don't want none of my younguns in that mill at all.

AMANDA KING

Greensboro, North Carolina

My mother left when I was born. She went to school in Durham and then she left. Because, you know, that was the time I call the migration, when a lot of black people from the South went North. She went up there because she thought she could get a better job. She'd come down and visit and from what I can remember I know I missed her and everything. I wanted her to come home. A couple times my grandparents took me up there to visit her and then the last time we drove up there, when I was five, they took me up there to stay.

Now my father, that's a different story. I never laid eyes on the man really. That was just something that happened to my mother and I came out of that. I was about twelve and I asked her about him once and she told me his name. Then we never said nothing about him no more. He knew I was there and if he had wanted to see me I guess he would have.

When I went up to New Jersey I was glad to be with my mother, but I was back with my grandparents in the South every summer. I think my mother went to Newark because, you know, the thing with my father and, you know, the big city was where the money was. She saw there was no future for her in the South and, like I said before, the land of opportunity was the North. I remember I didn't like it in Newark. The whole time I lived there until I was eighteen I didn't like it. Every time summer came 'round I was ready to go back down South. The whole time I was there I just didn't adapt to city life, but I had to stay there because of my mother. The first place we lived that I can remember real good was in this apartment building on Central Avenue. It was like groups of different kinds of people, Italians, blacks, Puerto Ricans, and so on. Everybody that lived on that street was poor. The apartment was like a walk-in and the bathroom was on the back porch. We had to take a bath in the kitchen. I thought we should have been back down South.

In Ahoskie, down South, we had lived in a black community. The town was three miles away. It was a small town much like it is now. Most of the industry was tobacco. The blacks owned a lot of things like the funeral homes and stores. Yeah, the blacks owned a lot of stuff in Ahoskie.

In Newark, as a kid growing up there, I didn't see it as bad or rough but it was. When I was growing up there it wasn't no big deal but now since I been away, I wouldn't dare go back there because it's awful. When we moved over to this street on Sussex Avenue, we got robbed like around three times but then it was no big deal. And the streets, they weren't safe, but if you lived there you learned to deal with it. I didn't get into the street scene. I went to school and came home. As a matter of fact, especially in high school, I was really quiet and shy. I didn't even go out or anything. I just had a few friends. We'd play in the front or back yard. It wasn't really no yard, just cement. There were two apartment buildings where I lived and there were about six families in each, so there were a lot of people to play with right there. In school, we didn't learn too much. I remember one time when I was in the third grade I saw this mother come and beat this teacher up. It was that kind of school. I seen that twice. When I was in high school I seen three guys beat up this teacher. We were changing classes and these guys just came in and started beating this teacher up. And we just sat there. It was like, what you going to do?

The only violence in my home was after my stepfather left and he saw that my mother could make it on her own and she didn't need him. Then he came back and he wanted to fight. We all fought that day. He was in there beating on her and so I was trying to beat him. That was the only time we knew about him beating her. But after he left she told us that he used to threaten her with a gun after we kids had already gone to bed. He'd come home drunk or whatever. Then this man was something. After he left, then here come all these kids saying, I'm your brother or sister. My mother knew that he had girlfriends and that he was messing around but she never told us.

Now my mother, let me tell you about my mother. She took care of us. We were brought up a lot better than other kids. When we were still young she worked. She went to work in the factory or whatever and I think she even worked for the telephone company one time. We always had food, we lived pretty good compared to the other kids in our neighborhood. My grandfather and grandmother brought her up to be independent, to take care of herself, to save money, 'til now she's doing all right. She works at the Federal Building now in Immigration. But she don't want to get married. She's independent and don't want to go through that no more.

After my stepfather left, it was, like, my mother and the kids. It wasn't like we all sat around and talked and thought about what we'd do whenever we grew up. We were just trying to survive. I never really even thought about being a mother. But coming up I think I really needed somebody. So when I did meet my daughter's father, I just latched onto him right then and there.

When I was coming up, my mother worked so I was the one that did the cleaning and the babysitting. On Saturdays she did the big cleaning and we'd all leave the house with our friends. My grandparents brought my mother up to be responsible and I think that's why, when she went to New Jersey, my stepfather latched onto her. Because he thought he had found a woman that would go out and work and take care of him, and he thought he had found a good thing. That's why when she got rid of him, he couldn't deal with it. He saw that she didn't need him.

I came back South to go to college. I didn't finish because I dropped out my second year. I should have stayed. After I graduated from high school I worked in a factory where they made Bingo games. Isn't that something? And it took me the longest time to find that job. But it was a job. At the time in Newark, they had a lot of programs to recruit students from the North who wanted to go to school but their parents didn't really have the money. This was something my mother found out about. You could go on a financial aid and work-study type thing. I think my mother wanted all of us kids to go to college. 'Cause when we were in school, she was really putting out the money for it. When I got a chance to go to Shaw College, I jumped at it because I saw a way of getting out of Newark and going back South.

When I first went I really wanted to go to college, but then I met my husband. We went together something like three months and then we jumped into this marriage thing. I don't really think we knew what we were doing. He was pretty nice and had a great family. I shouldn't be prejudiced, but here in the South it seems people can really push for what they want. They really go out and get what they want. That don't sound right now, does it? But, like his family, one sister is a principal of a school, his brother is a teacher, so like, they all did good. Seems like people in the city don't have too much hope or something. But we moved back to New Jersey and stayed about six months. Then me and my husband split up. Nikki, my daughter, was born up there and then I came back down here to Greensboro because I had relatives here.

When I first got back down here, I got a job in Cone Mills. My cousin was working there in the main office, so she kind of got everybody a job there. When I first started working there I did this job called filling batteries, working in the weave room. The first week was like this training period and then I was real happy to have a job. But when they took me up to the weave room and told me what I was going to be doing, well, I didn't like that too much. Because you had to have a lot of speed. You had to work fast for your own good because if you didn't the things would run out on you. And if they ran out on you then you had to work even faster to get them caught back up. It was like thirty-six or thirty-seven looms you had to keep up. It was mostly women in the weave room. You had your men fixers and stuff like that, but mostly it was women filling the batteries and weaving. The bosses were all men. You had women working in the offices, but there were no women bosses. There were more blacks than whites in the Revolution plant where I worked. Before I got fired, I was there for almost three years. No union. They had tried to unionize before but I had heard that just before the vote the Cones had gotten some men to scare them out of it. I got pieces of the story from the older workers. Then they had tried to unionize again and nothing happened with that. It kind of scared the people off. Then I joined the union organizing committee, the Revolution Organizing Committee or ROC.

This guy who lived next to me introduced me to some people who were working in the same mill that I was working in. I found out they were in the Revolution Organizing Committee, but at the time I didn't know they were in the Communist Workers Party. Sandi Smith, a black woman, was in charge of ROC. When I first met her she was nice and you could tell she was a go-getter. Everything she stood for she really believed.

See, what happened was that they wanted everybody to know that they were organizing a union so they had this meeting. The first time we went, there were a lot of people there, about two hundred. Everybody was really enthused because they were tired of the junk that the Cones were putting down. They had a packed crowd there that night. It was on a Sunday. Then this guy gets up and gives this communist speech, and people felt like they wanted a union but they didn't know about this communist business. So a lot of people didn't come back to the meetings. After the speech, though, I was ready to go for it. 'Cause I was tired of coming home, working so hard every day, having to take all this crap at work. They were coming down on you whenever they wanted to. It was always like, you had to speed up your work, and they were wanting to put more work on you. Stuff like that. The Cones could do any way they wanted to do with us. They were getting away with a lot of things. The supervisors could just come and talk to you any way they wanted to. The place was filthy and some people were talking about having brown lung. Then, like the people in the dye room messing with all that dye, they never knew what they were messing with—in a few years they might have skin cancer or something. They come out of there smelling bad. When I left I was only making about $3.60 an hour. That wasn't enough for what we were doing. No way. I was working the second shift in 1978 and we had up to thirty-eight looms that we had to keep up. No, $3.60 an hour wasn't nothing. I felt like a union could change a lot of that, because the Cones had the money. We thought if we could get a union we could get better working conditions, more pay, and a retirement plan.

Before I started running around with ROC people, though, I'm a kind of person that's hot-tempered, so if I thought I was getting a bad deal or something, I'd go to the supervisor. I think ROC knew I was like that because a couple of times they went with me up to the front office and they'd talk for me saying, yes, this woman's being treated this kind of way and that kind of way. Then I started passing out these union leaflets and the supervisor really stayed on me because they were trying to get all the people on the organizing committee fired. So I'd hand out leaflets in the morning and then when I went to work the supervisor started getting on me for just little things. There were a couple of people they had gotten rid of before me. So they were getting us one at a time. So when I came in they be on me all the time. They watched the weave room all the time, and if I wasn't there they'd have me in the office. For every little thing I was in the office. One time right before we went for vacation one supervisor just tried to talk me down, just really got on my case, got all up in my face because he knew I was hot-tempered and he thought I would come back at him. But I had to keep my cool because I had to keep my job.

I really did want a union and I did like running around with these certain people, but I didn't know about communism at the time. They were really into this Marxism, Leninism, Mao Zedong stuff and they were trying to get people like me to just grab it right then and there. They were trying to be my friends, doing stuff for me, and at the same time running this stuff through my head. I tried to read something by Mao and a book by Marx but it just didn't do nothing for me. Now I read some books by Malcolm X, Angela Davis, and Dick Gregory and I understood all that.

You know, the leaders of the ROC lost their jobs too, but it just seemed like they were used to losing their jobs. They had been in this in the sixties and seventies. This was like a lifelong thing for them, to get out there and protest. They were like, what do you call them—intellectuals. That's what the whole thing was about. You got the ones that go to university that are supposed to make all the speeches, they're the ones that are supposed to lead, you know, put this little revolution together, and then you got the little ones, you know the ones that go to work in the factory every day, they be the ones that have to fight. I had a child and I thought I don't have the time to be running around with these people. I mean I could see it if I were back in high school or college, back when I really wanted to change the world. You couldn't have stopped me then. But shoot, I mean I understand some of that stuff they were talking about, like the bourgeoisie, the rich and the poor and all that, but I had surviving on my mind for me and my kid. I just couldn't cope with all that stuff too. Then I was fired on November 7, 1978.

After that, one of the women in the group claimed that I had said something against the Communist Workers Party. Well, I probably had said something, but what kind of damage could I do? Now I'm going to tell you something. The people that I met had been in so many different groups. A bunch of them had been in this group, a bunch of them had been in that group, political organizations, and this one didn't work out so they went to another group, and that didn't work out and so they went on to another one. Now the Communist Workers Party was against this other communist group called the Revolutionary Communist Party. So it was like a constant battle. Somebody from the RCP, this woman I worked with, was always in my ear talking about the RCP, trying to get me against the CWP, and the CWP was always

Amanda King with her daughter, Nikki King, 1984.
Photo by the author.

talking against the RCP because they didn't like each other. And I was saying, "Now look, y'all supposed to stand for the same thing, why y'all can't get together and get something going? Y'all supposed to be fighting the same enemy, right?" Still it was like this hatred between them. See, it was like this one girl that I worked with she hated this other girl that was in the RCP. She was always talking to me about this other girl and she wanted me to hate her too, and I said, "Look, I'm not going to hate her because you dislike her views." This was one thing I was always saying to them, "I don't understand, 'cause y'all are against the same enemy, how y'all ever going to get a revolution going if you can't even get yourselves going right?"

See that's something I still don't understand. You still got so many communist-type organizations. They were both trying to organize the textile mills but they were constantly putting out leaflets against each other. They'd say, don't believe what the RCP is doing, they doing so-and-so, believe us. After a while I didn't care one way or the other. One group was always pitting you against another group. One group would invite me to their house for a meeting and the other would say, "Come on over to our house, we're going to be having a meeting over here," and I'd go in there and they'd be making jokes about the other group. I'm serious, it was just pure hatred. And I thought, "God, y'all ain't never gonna get no revolution going." And I'm saying, "Well the Man know y'all ain't got nothing together, so he ain't got nothing to worry about." They had groups all around and they all broke up because they all wanted to be the leader. That was one thing that I did realize about them all was that it was a bunch of bull. You know, like they ain't never gonna get it together because there was just too much hatred.

I was approached one time and asked if I wanted to join the Communist Workers Party. But now you look at the ones that got killed. Most of them weren't even from poor working-class backgrounds. They were all doctors and stuff like that. Some of them had graduated from Duke. What they asking me to join a communist party for? Here I don't know nothing about stuff like that.

CRYSTAL LEE SUTTON

Graham, North Carolina

My first job in the mill was filling batteries. This older woman trained me because she was working her notice. I remember my first day it was so noisy in there and it was so dusty, that I got to crying because I couldn't hear. And I felt like I had gotten all stopped up from the lint, so we went to the bathroom to eat our supper. This woman was talking to me and she asked me if I went to school and I told her where I went to school and what grade I was in. Her name was Mrs. Johnson and so she said she had a son named Henry who was in the same grade I was in. And I said, "Yeah, I know Henry. He was my boyfriend when we first moved to Burlington." She said, "Please don't tell any of the kids at school that I'm working here 'cause I wouldn't want to embarrass him." And I thought to myself, she had the audacity to say that to me and here I was a teenager working in the mill taking over her job.

But I never said anything to her about it and I never mentioned it at school either. I felt like if she didn't want me to I wouldn't. Henry was a very smart boy and I felt like he came from a well-off family. That was just the impression I got, he never was conceited or anything, but usually the smarter kids came from the families with a little bit more money than the average textile worker's kids. The reason I think that is because those parents probably had more schooling and, because they had more money, they had the time to take with their children instead of working all the time. I always got the feeling when I was in school that textile work was something to be looked down on because like, the first day of school you had to tell what your mama and daddy did. I wasn't ashamed of what they did but I would rather not been asked because there were doctors' children in the room and all. You just got the feeling that the teacher just didn't want to hear the fact that your parents worked in the textile mills. I just rather it had been left alone. I didn't think what my parents did really mattered that much. That was just a feeling I had at a very young age. The doctors' children were always smarter than the mill children because when they were called on they knew to answer and the rest of us just wished that we could see through the void. When I went to work in the mill and Mrs. Johnson said what she did to me, I really figured all that out.

Filling batteries was dangerous work with the machines running and the shuttles going very fast. At the time I wore my hair very short, that was just a style I had picked up, and that was good because you come out of there covered with cotton dust and all. At the time I didn't realize how dangerous the work was. I knew that the floors were very oily and you'd see snakes every once in a while, but at the time I just figured that was the way a textile plant was. My wage was probably about a dollar an hour because before I was working for fifty cents an hour at a florist shop and I went to work in the mill because I could make more money. I took distributive education in high school, which meant that I got out of school at 12:30 and went to work in the mill on second shift full time. It was very hard trying to do your homework in the mill, studying Macbeth and all that crap. Where the hell has that done me any good? All I did was memorize enough to pass the test and then forget it. I had this friend that would come down and help me. We would work fast so we could take a break and go up there and get some ice cream so I could study.

Daddy always talked about education. He got real upset because he said that it didn't look like none of his children were going to graduate. So I was the first to graduate in 1959. The only reason I finished school was because of Daddy. I hated every second I went. I even hated study hall and lunch time. I hated it because of the way the teachers treated the working-class kids. I resented that, because I didn't feel like we could help what our parents did and I wasn't ashamed of my parents. I was always proud of them and I didn't think that it was right for the school system to judge us because of where our parents worked. I used to always be secretary or treasurer of something. I remember that first happening to me in the sixth grade. I was voted secretary. And it shocked me. I was in a state of shock the whole year because it always seemed like the higher class kids always got to do stuff like that. And they were always in the plays, cheerleaders, majorettes, they definitely dominated the school. I resented that very much. I felt like we needed more attention. There were different classrooms for the different students even back then and we mill kids just couldn't move as fast as the others. It was just impossible to do because we had to work, and we didn't have the help at home. Both my parents only had about an eighth-grade education. So they couldn't very well help a lot. I just hated it.

When I was in the eighth grade I really wanted to quit. I really got this desire to go in the service, and it upset Mama. Now Daddy went along with me because he knew Mama would ab-solutely refuse to allow it. I finally figured that out when I got a little older, because Mama said only whores went into the army. So I gave up that desire. But I wanted to go into the service to get away from everything, to travel, and to be myself.

I was almost eighteen when I got married. After Mama put a halt to me going into the service, that was all I ever thought about was getting married and getting away from home. I never even thought about getting my own place to myself. I had a job, but I thought I had to get married to get out. I wanted to be a beautician. I really wanted to be a beautician. So I checked around and there was this woman in the neighborhood who had a beauty shop a couple of blocks from us and she told me where to write to for some information. The nearest school was in Raleigh and I just knew that Daddy couldn't afford to send me because I would have to have a place to stay, so I gave up on that idea.

Mark, my son, was three years old when his daddy got killed, and I moved back in with Mama and Daddy. No, we were already living with Mama and Daddy when my husband got killed because me and Junior had had a lovers' spat. We were mature in a lot of ways, but we were real jealous, and he liked to take some drinks sometimes. Glenraven Mills where he was working at had a Christmas dinner just for the workers, or that's what Junior told me, and I worked all day long cleaning up that house from top to bottom, I wanted to go to that dinner that night. But he said it was only for the employees. At midnight he still wasn't home and I was fuming. So we had a spat which ended up with him shoving a gun in my face. The bullet didn't hit me, but when the gun went off it broke my nose. So then I went home to Mama and Daddy. We were in the process of getting back together when he got killed in a car accident.

I was about twenty then, and to get my insurance money Daddy had to be my guardian. That was so damn strange, here I was married, widowed, and a mother, and I couldn't even write my own checks. I thought that was stupid. Then Mark was about six months old when I went to work for Southern Life Insurance and I would take him to the babysitter's. After that I went back into the mill and got fired because I refused to check a man that was running. I was pregnant with Jay at the time, and I refused to run behind that man and check him. I tried to tell him, you work at a speed that you can work at five and six days a week. Don't speed up, work at a normal pace. The faster you go the more work they gonna put on you. And I think he got pissed because I had to check him, but that was my job, and I got fired because I finally refused to check him. That was at Glenraven Mills. Then Jay was born in 1962. Jay was six months old when I moved to Roanoke Rapids and I met Cookie Jordan. We married shortly after that. Then Elizabeth was born in 1965. She was probably two when I went to work as a waitress.

I had taken a course on how to be a waitress and had gotten a certificate. They were having this teacher over at the Holiday Inn. I went six weeks training to be a waitress. My sister Seretha was working as a waitress at the restaurant and she got me the job. I worked there a pretty good while and I really enjoyed that type of work. But then I wanted to get on at JP Stevens because they paid more money.

I started trying and it took me about two years to get on. What happened was that we moved out to Henry Street and it was a dead end. Two boss men lived on my street and there was a woman who lived behind me that had been at JP Stevens maybe five or six years. She talked for me and Seretha, who was already working at Stevens, talked for me, and then I called both of those boss men. I talked to them personally and finally got hired. So I went to work at JP Stevens in 1972. I was a gift-set operator. You know, like you go to Sears or somewhere and you see these towels fixed in pretty boxes. That was my job, to fold those towels, put pasteboard in them, fold them a certain size and put them in the boxes, put Saran Wrap over them and pack them. I was probably making $2.25 an hour at that time. That was better than waitressing because I was just making a dollar an hour plus tips. Yeah, that was a lot better. I was also working part-time at Hornes Restaurant.

Then, when Ralph Sizemore opened up a nightclub, he asked me to run it for him. So I worked my notice at the mill, and then when I was going to leave, my boss man told me that if I got over there and didn't like it, he'd give me my job back. So I loved the work at the club and some of my boss men from the mill would even come over, but Cookie bitched about me doing it so much that I finally told James, my boss man, "Reckon you'd give me my job back?" So I went back on the very same shift doing the very same work. Then I worked there until I was terminated in 1973. I was terminated for union activity. I attended my first union meeting on Mother's Day in 1973 and on May 30th I was fired. Less than a month since I attended my first union meeting.

Nobody really approached me about the union. I had been out on sick leave. I had hurt my foot. My sister worked right down from me and she came up and said, "Lee, somebody was handing out union cards but don't you take one 'cause if you do you'll be fired." I said, "Who's handing them out?" She said, "I don't know but don't you take one." Then she went on back there to her job.

So I started asking different ones around and nobody would say nothing. So I asked this older woman, "Do you know anything about this union stuff?" And she said, "Lee, all I know is there's a notice about this meeting on the bulletin board." So I took a piece of paper and wrote down the place, it was going to be at a church, and the time. So I started to talk to different ones about if they were going and nobody said nothing, so I asked my friend Liz. I said, "Liz, how about going with me to that union meeting?" She had three little girls. She said, "Lee, I don't have nobody to keep the kids." I said, "Oh, Cookie will keep the children."

I never will forget, I went to Burlington that Saturday on Mother's Day, and Mama got mad with me 'cause I left early to go to that union meeting. She didn't think I ought to go. But I went over to JB Younts, he had been a real close friend, and I knew he knew about unions and all because I remember he tried to get Daddy to join the union at Cone Mills. He told me, "Lee, you do everything you can to try to get that union in." He said, "You get home in time to go to that union meeting." So I did. I never will forget it. Liz and I pulled up at this church—it was a black church—and I had never seen so many blacks in all my life. Liz said, "You sure you want to do this?" and I said, "Well, we're here. We might as well go on in." So we went in and there were maybe four or five other white people there. We went down and sat on the front row 'cause I didn't want to miss out on nothing. After the meeting, I agreed to go into the mill wearing a union button to try to get the union in. We were real strong with the blacks but we were weak with the whites. So I knew a lot of people I was going to talk with.

Eli Zivkovitch was the organizer. He was from Fairfield, Virginia, an ex–coal miner. He and his family were so poor that at one time they lived in a tent. He was a very handsome man, and I really loved my daddy more than anything in this world, but Eli was like what I wish my daddy had 'a been as far as being more modern, like realizing that women had more worth in this world than just being a sex object. That women had brains and that they should use those brains. It was okay for women to do so-called men's work. The men I had met before had always seemed to be more concerned with a woman's outward appearance. Eli was a good man, a fighter and a survivor. Hours meant nothing to him as far as his work went. He was not a nine-to-five person. He was available when you needed him, and that's the way he taught me to work. Eli said we could talk union and hand out literature on our break time in the canteens. So I got people to join the union real quick like.

Then they started calling me into the office. I had never been called into the office to be talked to about anything. But all of a sudden I couldn't do nothing right. Talking too much, standing in the bathroom too much. Nothing had changed, that was just their agitation trying to get me to quit trying to organize. Eli had give us this book called *What the Company Will Do for You*. It was all blank pages. He told us if they called us in the office for us to write down what they said. Because if they had a right to write us up, we had a right to write them up. I always took my pencil and my little book and I would write down things that was happening. This blew the boss men's mind. They couldn't believe I was doing this.

Then what happened was that the company posted a notice on the bulletin board and it was, in effect, trying to scare people. It stated something like it was going to be an all black union. Eli said he needed a copy of it to send to the National Labor Relations Board. So different people said they would copy the letter, you know, but whenever they tried they were told they would be fired. So one day, Eli said, "Crystal, I've got to have a copy of that letter." I said, "Okay." So I went up to the bulletin board and I was trying to copy the letter and the boss man came up and said, "You can't copy that, if you do you'll be fired." I went back to Eli that night and said, "Man, they said they'll fire us." He said, "I'm telling you it's your constitutional right," and he said, "I need a copy of that letter." I said, "I'll get a copy of that letter today." So I went on into work and, lo and behold, they had tables set up with tablecloths on them. They were having a safety dinner for us.

When the company claimed that they had no lost time for accidents they'd give us a little old dinner. But I've actually seen people with an arm in a cast sitting in the office. Prior to the union, we thought they were doing us a favor by letting us come in, sit in the office, and pay us. We didn't know nothing about workmen's compensation.

So I went to the pay phone which the company had conveniently installed to keep us out of the office. They had said we could use it any time we wanted to and I had done so. If there had been a storm, I'd call home to make sure the kids were all right and all. So I called Eli and said, "Look man, I can't copy that letter tonight because we're having a safety supper." 'Course he had to know what that was, so I quickly explained it to him. So I said, "Anyway, Eli, I'm hungry and I want to eat my supper." But he said, "Look Crystal, you can afford to lose a few pounds and I need that letter." He knew he had made me mad then, so I said, "I'll get that damn letter."

So I started talking around and I came up with this idea. I went over to the ones that were in the union and I said, "Look, Eli needs that letter so I'll tell you what let's do. I'll memorize the first two lines of it and go in the bathroom and write it down. Mary, you memorize the next two" and I told all of them the lines of the paragraph to remember. Well, it got to be a big joke because we were pretending like we were getting water, you know, and trying to read the letter too. But we couldn't remember what we had read by the time we got to the bathroom. So we all got to laughing about it. So I said, "Hell, I got to get that letter." So I said to my sister, she was a service person, I said, "Seretha, I need a clipboard." She said, "What you going to do?" I said, "I'm going to get that letter." We didn't have no set time for a break, they said they would motion for us when it was our turn to go eat. Seretha said, "Oh God," but she gave me a clipboard.

As soon as they motioned for us, I took the clipboard and went immediately to the bulletin board and started to write. Because of the supper, everyone from management was at this dinner. So they took turns coming up to me telling me that I couldn't copy that letter. If I did, I'd be fired. Then the big man come up and he called me Lee. His name was Mason Lee. I said, "Mr. Lee, I didn't know you knew my name." And he said, "Yeah, I know who you are." He told me that if I didn't leave he was going to call the police to come in there and take me out. I said, "Mr. Lee, sir, you do what you want on your break time, you even get to go out for supper, and we can't even sit on the steps. This is my break time and I'm telling you I'm going to copy this letter. It's my constitutional right." So I continued to write and my knees were shaking like I was going to collapse any minute. I said, "If you do call the cops, you're going to have to call the Chief of Police because my husband is a jealous man and he won't let me ride home with just anybody." I thought to myself I'm going to put him to the test. I'm just going to push him and see what he does do.

So I copied the letter and folded it up and stuck it down my bra figuring, well, nobody will get it down there. I went on down there and got me a plate and went to this special canteen that the company had installed within the last month. They no longer let the ones in my department go to the old canteen. As soon as we got into work we had to report to the new canteen. Right there within twenty steps of my job they built this canteen. They went to that much trouble to separate me from the rest of the workers. And I went in there and everybody said, "God, you got more guts, what did they say?" I gave my dinner to some man in there and said, "Well as soon as they blow the whistle, they'll come and get me. Mr. Lee said they were going to fire me and call the police. So y'all can expect anything."

I went back out there when I figured break was about up, put on my lipstick, and was acting real cool, calm and collected, when we all started back to work. Then here they come. Three of them. "Mr. Lee wants to see you in the office." So I said, "Seretha don't you let nobody mess with my pocketbook, I'll be back shortly." "All right," she said. So they took me up to the door of the main office and pushed a button and the door came open and they took me in there where they were all sitting at a big table and

Mason Lee was sitting at the head. He started talking to me and I said, "Mr. Lee, sir," I had me a pencil and a piece of paper, I said, "Before you tell me anything you going to have to tell me all your names and how to spell them." So he started to spell his name and then he stopped and said, "I don't have to do that."

Then he started telling me all the things that I had done wrong. Said I had stayed in the bathroom too long, used the pay phone when I wasn't supposed to, and, you know, all different kinds of reasons. He was talking so much I remember putting my hands on my ears and thinking, here is all these people in here that I have served at the restaurant, a couple of them I'd danced with, and my floorlady who had had me call my husband and get him to bring chicken up to the mill for us. All these people knew he was lying but didn't a one of them have the guts to say so. None of them said, "Mr. Lee you're lying, she used that phone on her break time, she was told she could use it." Nobody said nothing. I said, "I don't have anything to say. There is nobody in here on my side. Y'all are all company people and no matter what I say, y'all are going to be right and I'm going to be wrong." So then he said, "You going to have to leave the plant." And I said, "I don't have no way to go home, I didn't drive the car today, I got a ride with my sister." He said, "You call your husband to come and get you." And I said, "My husband's at work." So he said, "You call you a taxi." I said, "I don't have any money. You got to let me go back out there and get my pocketbook." Then he told Tommy Gardner, he said, "You go out there and get her pocketbook." I said, "If anybody touches my pocketbook, I'm going to have a warrant taken out on them for stealing." Finally, he said, "Let her back out there to get her pocketbook."

They went through the door with me and I went on around there and this black woman, Mary Moses, said, "What happened?" I said, "He fired me." Then I said, "Mary, give me your magic marker." So I grabbed it and I took a piece of pasteboard and I wrote the word UNION on it and, for some reason, I don't know why I did it, I climbed on the table and I just slowly turned the sign around. Everybody was in a state of shock and the machines started shutting down and everything got quiet. People started giving me the V sign. Then different ones from management came down there and tried to get me down off the table. Even my sister came down there. She said, "Lee, get down off that table and let me call Cookie to come and get you." Then I said to the boss man, "It's not their break time. Y'all gonna have to fire all of them too." Then sure enough here comes the chief of police. I got off the table and walked over there and he said, "Lee, what's wrong?" I said, "The man fired me and he fired me because I been trying to get the union in." He said, "Come on, let me take you home." I said, "You gonna take me home?" and he said, "Yeah." I said, "I want you to put that in writing." And I handed him a piece of paper and he started to write, and then he balled it up and said, "I don't have to do that." Then he grabbed me and literally forced me out of the gate and I was trying to get back in. I was fighting. It was a damn good thing I didn't know karate or he would have had to shoot me, and would have probably gotten away with it. They forced me in the car and took me to jail and locked me up.

I remembered from watching Perry Mason that they had to allow me to make one phone call. So that's all I'd say. He asked me my name (he knew my name, he lived a block over from me and he was my first cousin's husband) and I'd say, "All I got to say is that you supposed to allow me one phone call." So he did and when he did, I called the union office. Eli wasn't in but the other organizer was and she knew where he was, she'd get in touch with him, and they'd be down there just as soon as they could. Well, he took me in there and he's the one that locked me up, shoved me in the cell and locked me up. The women's section of the jail was away from the other part and it was beginning to get dark outside. It was filthy in there. I started crying because I thought nobody really knows where I am. I didn't know whether Eli was going to come or not. I was thinking what effect this was going to have on the kids when the other children found out that their mama had been in jail.

Well, it seemed like forever, but Eli did come. He offered me a cigarette. He squatted down and I was laying on the bed crying. I said, "Eli, you know I don't smoke." Then he walked over and said, "Open this damn door and let her out." Boy, that chief of police put the key in there and he opened that damn door too. The next day Eli went down there with this other organizer from out of town and they met with the city manager and the chief of police and the big people in town and Eli told them that this International would not tolerate such actions, that they were liable to be sued for conspiracy with the companies. And we had no more trouble with them. Prior to that they would circle the hotel where the union office was, watching us, spying on us all the time. But after that, there was not any violence in that campaign whatsoever.

That night Cookie came up to the hotel and Eli explained what happened. Well now, Jay had been born illegitimately and I had always wanted to tell the boys they had different daddies. I wanted my children to know. But Cookie refused to allow me to do so. He had said they didn't have to know things like that. I just knew that when they grew up they would find out and they would hate me for it. If they thought I'd lie to them about that I'd lie to them about anything. So I just told Cookie, I said, "Well, nobody will ever have anything to hold over me no more." So I woke the children up and I always kept pictures of their daddy and legal papers in a file box. So I took the pictures out and I told Mark that his real daddy was dead, and I told Jay that he had a different daddy. That was the best thing I ever did in my life. I did it because I had been taken to jail and I figured somebody would be cruel enough to get that stuff going with the children in school. And I wanted my children to hear it from me. It set me free, it really did. The children accepted it. They were probably still a little young, but I think it made them even closer to each other. Until this day they're really close. That really set me free, because then I had nothing to hide, nothing to be afraid of.

After that I got even more deeper involved with the union campaign. I was fired in 1973 but didn't get reinstated 'til 1978. My case went as high as the second circuit court in New York

Crystal Lee Sutton, 1984.
Photo by the author.

City. And it took that many years before a decision was made. Joseph Williams was a black man who was fired before me and he was also reinstated three weeks before me. He was also fired for union activity. He still works in the plant in Patterson.

Eli was always coming up with these ideas, like, if he had to go out of town he would ask me to keep the office open because he felt that people should know that somebody was there. We moved from this little room in the hotel to this bigger room. So I kept things going. If people came in with a problem I'd take a statement from them and was always available.

Then he came up with this bright idea. He thought we should have some cheerleaders and I said, "Oh God, Eli, I don't have time to do all this stuff. Cookie's already fussing that I spend too much time at the union office now." But anyway I started talking to the children about it and they were all excited about it. So at one time I had about twenty cheerleaders. I made all the outfits for them. The idea was to get their parents involved with the union. They cheered outside at the meetings and stuff like that. It was very effective.

Then Christmastime came and Eli decided we needed a float for the Christmas parade. That was a hassle because those in charge of the parade didn't want us to have a union float. So we went around to try to find a float and naturally Eli was out of town again. So I got some women and men together and we decided it would be cheaper to rent a float than to try to fix one up. So we went down there and put our name in the pot and then had to go down there and see someone in Roanoke Rapids, some higher-ups, for them to agree to let us be in the parade. I made clown suits and got the cheerleaders and the float ready and none of us mothers had ever been cheerleaders or been on a float. Then what was the most confusing thing was getting them to march, but we got it together. We sang Christmas songs like "Silent Night" and "Santa Claus is Coming to Town," and stuff like that. This was about six months into the union drive. At that time I was on unemployment and they ruled in my favor 'cause I just explained that I got fired for union activity. The company just did me a favor because that just gave me more time to work for the union. I never will forget all those patterns we cut out for those cheerleader outfits, but we finally got them sewed up in time for Christmas. That was an exciting part of my life because I was doing something I didn't even think I could do.

I worked full-time like that for the union up until Eli resigned. He was mentally and physically worn out. He was there for one year. An organizer's life is hard and can be very lonely. It's twenty-four hours and seven days a week. You deal with the workers but you don't have anybody to talk to about your own problems. Workers tend to forget that organizers are human beings also, that we too have families. They forget that we breathe and bleed the same way they do. I really hated to see Eli leave the campaign but I knew that he had done what he said he would do. He had said, "I told y'all the day I came here that I had never lost an election and didn't intend to lose this one. Now I've done all that I can do and the International has sent in other organizers." He needed to be with his family. He probably didn't go home but three or four times and then just for a few days the whole time he was here. He gave his whole self to that campaign. Then when he resigned, I continued talking union and stuff like that, but I wouldn't go to the union office because I felt like the new organizers resented me because Eli and I were so close. And I felt like a lot of them had backstabbed Eli, that they had not supported him like they should have throughout the campaign.

Then I stayed with Cookie until 1976 when he said he had had enough. He didn't want me to get involved with the union from the very beginning and I resented that because there he was at the paper mill making about twelve dollars an hour and he was a shop steward. He said if I got involved I'd get fired. He'd pick me up at work and say, "Well, you made it through one more day." And I'd say, "Why you keep saying I'm going to get fired? I'm not the only person in the union." And he'd say, "Because I know how you are. When you believe in something you give it all you got." He'd say, "You gonna get fired." And he was right. He wasn't shocked when I got fired. Even though he helped with the cleaning and he learned to iron, he would throw my union work up to me. And I said, "Hell, let the housework go, I'll do it some time. I can do it, I don't need sleep. I can sleep when I'm dead." I just didn't need that kind of crap. So we had an election in 1974 and we won, but we didn't get a contract until October 19, 1980. That's because JP Stevens was found guilty so many times of bargaining unfairly. They had to go through all that in court before they would sit down and bargain for a contract. It took six years to get that contract.

Right after I got fired, Henry Liebframan, a free-lance journalist, heard that a campaign was going on and he came to Roanoke Rapids and talked to Eli. He had been reading about the campaign and heard that textile workers were better off now than they had been in the thirties. He didn't believe that, because he had some family in a plant here, so he wanted to do an article for the *New York Times Magazine*. So Eli said, "You probably want to talk to Crystal because she just got fired." So he interviewed me and he wrote the article for the *New York Times*. It was such a success that the Macmillan Publishing Company asked him to write a book and so he wrote his first book, *Crystal Lee: A Woman of Inheritance*. I agreed to let him do it and Eli was real excited about it because he explained to me about how important it was for union people to learn about unions, doing education work and everything. So I agreed for him to do the book. The book came out in 1975. I'll never forget 'cause one of my first boyfriends, Gilbert Newsome, had a commercial going on the television. He was working at the tire place then, and they were advertising the book *Crystal Lee: A Woman of Inheritance*. I got a big kick out of that. I was proud to have lived long enough to see something I believe in do people good.

It was interesting, too, that a movie was actually made of my life. Mama had always wanted one of us to win the Miss America pageant or something and I thought this was even better than winning a beauty pageant. I felt like my daddy would've been real proud of me. When he first got me the job in Cone Mills, he said, "Now honey, they got a union down there but you don't have nothing to do with it or you'll be fired." And I was brought up to believe in what my daddy said. I never questioned it. I just remember seeing this woman. I found out she was a shop steward, and she was always laughing, carrying on, having a good time. And I said, "What in the world she always going to the office for," and they said she was taking care of union business. And I remember thinking, what in the world could be so bad about having a union when she was having such a good time. But I never asked anybody about it and they never tried to get me to join the union there. I guess they figured that if my parents were anti-union, they figured I probably would be too. What changed my mind about that was living with Cookie Jordan, listening to his meetings and him being a shop steward. He was making more money, had his birthday off, had decent insurance. I thought if he could be in a union, I didn't see why textile workers couldn't have a union too, and make those wages and have some of those benefits.

When I heard about them wanting to make a movie, the author called me about it and I wanted script rights, because you can see sex and violence anytime you cut the TV on. I said it had to be about the union. I said that rinky-dink stuff wasn't important. So he told them and they said that, naw, they couldn't do that, you know, give me script rights. So I said, "I don't need the publicity so tell them they can't do it." But they did anyway and I didn't make a cent on it.

I understand the political situation now better than I did before. I understand the need to be involved with politics. Politics is what makes this world go 'round. It is the ruling factor in why the poor continue to be poor and the rich continue to be rich. This bothers me a lot. Textile workers in North Carolina are the lowest paid and the least unionized in the South, where the labor struggle is hard and is getting harder every day. I attribute that to people we have in Congress. The Republicans. I understand the importance of history, which I didn't when I was in school. See, the only thing I learned in school about the unions was in economics. I still have my economics book at home and it had three little pages on unions. I remember my teacher when she taught about the unions, she talked about the blacks, the "niggers" as she called them, concentrated on driving big fancy cars and living in shacks. But Cookie Jordan always said I was color blind, that I couldn't tell one color from another. That was another reason he was against me going to that union meeting, because it was going to be in a black church. He was definitely, wholly, against it, but thank God I'm color blind.

Still my kids have only those three pages on unions, about the boycotts and the strikes. There is still a real need for union education in the schools. That's why the struggle is so hard. In my life I haven't seen no difference in the lives of textile workers.

ACKNOWLEDGMENTS

I am truly indebted to the people who were a source of support as I figured out how to write an oral history and, at the same time, figured out who I was in the context of American history. The most outstanding of these staunch supporters was the Reverend Dr. Katie Cannon, without whose endless support and encouragement I could not have seen this manuscript through the final stages. In addition, because Dr. Cannon herself comes from a heritage of southern mill workers, she was invaluable in helping me understand what life was like for my black counterpart. Her insight was crucial to my understanding of the history of southern black women and her support was critical to seeing this project to fruition. I also want to thank Bonnie Lunt, Rachel Burger, Mae Browning, and Steven Osborn for helping me grow these last years and for being those rare friends whom I could trust with my life.

There were others who became involved with this project at critical points. Victoria Fortino, who traveled with me in 1982 to North Carolina and assisted with the interviewing. My friend Nikki King, who was eight years old at the time, was a daily source of laughter and affection. Janet Koenigsamen rescued me from exhaustion when I was working for both the Brown Lung Association and on the project. Jonathan Lange of the Amalgated Clothing and Textile Workers Union introduced me to many mill women and consistently believed in the project and my ability to carry it out. The Southern Oral History Program at the University of North Carolina at Chapel Hill, especially Dr. Jacquelyn Hall and Cliff Kuhn, was very useful in helping me understand oral history and the industrialization of North Carolina. Dr. Michael Harris of Brandeis University was a source of support throughout the whole eight years. Dr. Robin Cromptin of the Chinese University of Hong Kong and Dr. Curtis Wood of Western Carolina University helped me formulate the basic idea from which this project grew. Kenneth Chapman, an essential friend, remained loyal despite the hundreds of favors I asked of him. Cathy Anderson, Jean Martin, Jennifer Abod, Dr. Sondra Stein, Nancy Lattanzio, Janet Kahn, Cynthia Peters, and Melanie Marcus, who all read the manuscript at various stages, can never be thanked enough.

Finally, I want to thank Jean Hinton Rosner for taking me to the People's Republic of China and for helping me to develop the political consciousness that was the driving force behind this project; all the remarkable southern mill women who took time out from their demanding lives to talk to me; and the ILR Press, especially Holly Bailey and Frances Benson, for recognizing the value of this work and convincing me that dreaming is believing that what you're dreaming is possible.

INDEX

Index